The Best & Worst of Hockey Firsts

THE UNOFFICIAL GUIDE

The Unofficial Guide
THE BEST
& WORST OF
HOCKEY
FIRSTS

Don Weekes &
Kerry Banks

GREYSTONE BOOKS

Douglas & McIntyre Publishing Group

Vancouver/Toronto/Berkeley

For all the hockey wives married to hockey geeks like us.

Greystone Books
A division of Douglas & McIntyre Ltd.
2323 Quebec Street, Suite 201
Vancouver, British Columbia
Canada V5T 4S7
www.greystonebooks.com

NATIONAL LIBRARY OF CANADA CATALOGUING IN PUBLICATION DATA
Weekes, Don
  The best and worst of hockey firsts: the unofficial guide/Don Weekes &
  Kerry Banks

  Includes index.
  ISBN 1-55054-860-3
  1. Hockey—Miscellanea.   2. National Hockey League—Miscellanea.   I. Banks,
Kerry, 1952–   II. Title.
GV847.W355 2003   796.962'64   C2003-910653-5

Library of Congress information is available upon request

Editing by Anne Rose
Cover and interior design by Peter Cocking
Cover photo by Dale MacMillan/Bruce Bennett Studios
Typeset by Tanya Lloyd Kyi
Printed and bound in Canada by Friesens
Printed on acid-free paper
Distributed in the U.S. by Publishers Group West

We gratefully acknowledge the financial support of the Canada Council for the Arts, the British Columbia Arts Council, and the Government of Canada through the Book Publishing Industry Development Program (BPIDP) for our publishing activities.

DON WEEKES *is an award-winning television producer-director at* CTV *in Montreal. He has written numerous hockey trivia books.*
KERRY BANKS *is an award-winning magazine journalist. He is the author of 11 books, including* Pavel Bure: The Riddle of the Russian Rocket *and four titles in the* Hockey Heroes *series.*

Contents

Introduction   vii

REGULAR SEASON

1 Sixty Minutes   1
Historic games

2 Dollar Signs   13
The redline, blueline and bottom line

3 Tools of the Trade   25
Gear through the years

4 Smells Like Team Spirit   37
Franchise firsts

5 Northern Lights   47
Superstars and unsung heroes

6 Smoking Guns   59
Goal rush

7 Cooler Kings   71
Penalty titleholders

8 No Mercy   83
Team extremes

9 Pipe Dreams   93
Number one netminders

10 Crime Blotter   109
Busts and bad behaviour

11 The Big Picture   117
Media milestones

12 The Old Barn   131
Houses of the holy

13 Bench Wizards   139
Coaching capers

14 Milestone Men   151
Standards of excellence

15 Bragging Rights   161
Scoring champions

16 The Trophy Hunters   169
Individual awards and honours

PLAYOFFS

17 The Tradition Continues   181
Torch bearers

18 Sniper Fire   195
Postseason scoring feats

19 Keepers of the Flame   203
Guardian gods

20 Dancing with Destiny   211
Cup wins and close calls

Acknowledgements   220
Player and Coach Index   222

Introduction

Ask any champion which Stanley Cup was his favourite, and the response is usually a story about his first. The game's top snipers—Wayne Gretzky, Mario Lemieux and Steve Yzerman—have been to the winner's circle on several occasions, but confess the experience was extra special the initial time they skated around the rink with Lord Stanley's chalice held aloft.

The first-time experience is a concept that the hockey world, with its dogged emphasis on most, longest and fastest, has largely overlooked as a legitimate source of NHL records. Of course, not every first is followed by a second. No other team, for example, has ever copied the California Golden Seals' decision to don white skates in 1971–72, which helps explain why we opted to include some onlys and—just for balance—a few notable lasts.

During our research, we unearthed a wealth of tales about the game's greatest innovators, puck stoppers, scoring leaders and troublemakers, and even a few about those lucky SOBs who just happened to be in the right place at the right time. We also settled the scores on a few commonly accepted but erroneous hockey firsts, such as the first head coach to hire an assistant coach (Lynn Patrick, not Fred Shero), the first NHLer to appear on the cover of *Time* magazine (Lorne Chabot, not Davey Kerr) and the first penalty shot in a Cup final (1922 not 1937).

So, here you go: from Jean Béliveau, the only rookie to be the NHL's highest-paid player, to Andy Bathgate, the first pro to use a curved stick, to Kelly Hrudey, the first goalie to wear a helmet cam, to King Clancy, the last big leaguer to play every position in one game. You'll find these and hundreds more in the first book ever published on NHL firsts, lasts and onlys: *The Best and Worst of Hockey Firsts: The Unofficial Guide.*

DON WEEKES & KERRY BANKS
June 2003

CHAPTER 1

Sixty
minutes

The NHL began play December 19, 1917, with two 60-minute tilts, as the Montreal Wanderers topped the Toronto Arenas 10–9 and the Montreal Canadiens beat the Ottawa Senators 7–4. The Wanderers' game drew a mere 700 fans. It was a bad omen. Two weeks later, fire ravaged the Wanderers' arena and the franchise folded, threatening the NHL's existence.

First NHL game played in two 25-minute periods
Montreal vs. Boston, September 26, 1995

This unusual format was used for the last NHL game played at Boston Garden, a preseason contest between the Bruins and the Canadiens billed as "The Last Hurrah." At half-time, Boston honoured its old opponents, including such guests as Jean Béliveau, Stan Mikita, Maurice Richard and Frank Mahovlich. At the game's conclusion, past Bruins greats were fêted, including Normand Leveille, whose promising career ended when he suffered a brain aneurysm in 1982. Helped by Ray Bourque, Leveille took a final, emotional skate around the Garden.

First NHL game played outdoors
Los Angeles vs. NY Rangers, September 27, 1991

The setting was Las Vegas. In a bizarre promotional venture, the Kings and Rangers played a preseason evening game at an outdoor rink set up in the parking lot of Caesar's Palace. The temperature hovered around 29°C for the desert duel. Besides slushy ice, the major hazard was grasshoppers. Attracted by the lights, the winged insects kept falling onto the rink. But the most embarrassing moments came when the players had to walk through the crowded casino in their robes to return to their rooms and shower.

First game cancelled due to rain
Detroit vs. San Jose, March 10, 1995

Rainouts are normally associated with baseball, but this NHL match was postponed when heavy rains caused the Guadalupe River to overflow its banks, creating flood conditions in San Jose. All roads leading to the Compaq Center were turned into rivers.

First game cancelled due to fog

Detroit vs. Boston, November 10, 1948

Unseasonably warm temperatures caused a fog bank to form inside steamy Boston Garden. Because of the poor visibility, referee Bill Chadwick halted the match after nine minutes of the first period. The game was replayed the next night, minus the fog. Boston won 4–1.

First game cancelled due to a fallen scoreboard

Boston vs. Buffalo, November 16, 1996

The huge, eight-sided scoreboard at Buffalo's Marine Midland Arena plummeted to the ice with a tremendous crash when a cable snapped during a maintenance check. The accident occurred only 90 minutes after the Boston Bruins had finished morning practice. Luckily no one was injured. The mishap caused cancellation of that night's game between the Bruins and Sabres.

Only game suspended due to a curfew

Boston vs. Toronto, March 31, 1951

Game 2 of the Bruins–Leafs 1951 semifinal never ended. It was called at 11:45 p.m. after one period of overtime, with the two clubs locked in a 1–1 tie. The province of Ontario had a Sunday curfew, which banned sporting events after midnight. The game ran long because it was so violent—play had to be halted several times to allow rink attendants to scrape blood off the ice. The game was ruled a no-contest, and Toronto went on to win the series four games to one.

Only game suspended due to a power failure

Edmonton vs. Boston, May 24, 1988

A transformer blew at Boston Garden at 16:37 of the second period of Game 4 of the finals, with the score tied 3–3. Despite the technicians' best efforts, power could not be restored. The game was ruled null and void, though player stats were counted. When the game was replayed two days later in Edmonton, the Oilers won 6–3, earning them the peculiar distinction of being the first team to sweep a Cup final in five games.

First game delayed by an announcement of war
Chicago vs. Boston, December 9, 1941
This clash between the Bruins and the Blackhawks was delayed while U.S. president Franklin Delano Roosevelt announced to the nation that war had been declared against Japan. More than 10,000 fans soberly listened to the 28-minute radio broadcast, as players from both teams sat on their respective benches, wrapped in blankets.

Last game played using only one puck
Los Angeles vs. Minnesota North Stars, November 10, 1979
No high-rising slappers, no deflected shots, no errant ricochets. In 1979, the Kings and the North Stars played an entire 60 minutes without the puck leaving the rink. That rare chunk of vulcanized rubber is now displayed in the Hall of Fame.

First forfeited game
Montreal Wanderers vs. Toronto Arenas, January 5, 1918
After the Wanderers' arena burned down January 2 and the club folded, the league awarded forfeit wins to the Wanderers' next two opponents: the Toronto Arenas and the Montreal Canadiens. To ensure it received credit for its victory and to pave the way for a lawsuit against Montreal for the default, Toronto proceeded with its "game" despite the lack of opposition. At 8:05 p.m., six Toronto players—including goalie Harry Homes—took to the ice at Mutual Arena. An NHL referee dropped the puck, and

Cy Denneny carried it down the ice and shot it into the empty net. Toronto got the 1–0 forfeit.

Last forfeited game
Detroit vs. Montreal, March 17, 1955

Habs supporters arrived at the Montreal Forum in an ugly mood after hearing NHL president Clarence Campbell had suspended superstar Maurice Richard for the rest of the season—and the playoffs—for punching linesman Cliff Thompson during a March 13 game. Campbell made a bad situation worse by showing up in person at the St. Patrick's Day game, giving fans a target for their fury. During the first intermission, Campbell was pelted with tomatoes and a tear gas canister went off. The fire marshal ordered the Forum cleared, and the game was suspended; Campbell ruled the game forfeited and awarded the win to the Red Wings. Montreal fans were not amused when Detroit went on to beat the Richard-less Canadiens in seven games in the Cup finals.

First game to finish in a tie
Toronto St. Pats vs. Ottawa, February 11, 1922
From 1917–18 to 1920–21, regular-season games were played until a winner was decided, no matter how long it took. In 1921–22, the league ruled that if a game remained tied after 20 minutes of overtime, it would end in a tie. The Senators and the St. Pats fought to the first NHL draw, a 4–4 overtime deadlock.

First scoreless game
Hamilton Tigers vs. Ottawa, December 17, 1924
It wasn't until the NHL's seventh season that a game ended in double zeroes. Hamilton's Jake Forbes and Ottawa's Alex Connell posted shutouts in a scoreless overtime draw.

First penalty-free game

Hamilton Tigers vs. Montreal, January 31, 1923
The Canadiens beat the Tigers 5–4 in this hockey no-hitter.

Only scoreless, penalty-free game

Chicago vs. Toronto, February 20, 1944
Goalies Mike Karakas and Paul Bibeault recorded goose eggs
and Bill Chadwick refereed as the Blackhawks and Leafs skated
through the only scoreless, penalty-free game in NHL annals in
a rapid one hour and 55 minutes.

First consecutive penalty-free games by a team

Toronto Maple Leafs, 1940–41
This Hap Day-coached team is the only one in history to play
back-to-back games without a penalty being called on either
team. On January 9, 1941, the Leafs beat the New York Rangers
3–2. On January 11, they routed the New York Americans 9–0.

First game in which a team was penalized for celebrating a goal

Toronto vs. Vancouver, February 22, 1993
When Glenn Anderson beat Vancouver Canucks goalie Kirk
McLean on a third-period breakaway, it gave him 1,000 career
points. His teammates jumped on the ice and mobbed him,
which prompted referee Denis Morel to give Toronto a delay-of-
game penalty. Because the Leafs led 7–1 at the time, coach Pat
Burns could afford to laugh. Sporting a wide grin, he assigned
Anderson to serve the minor.

First game in which a team was penalized for violating the NHL's hurry-up rule for face-offs and line changes

Phoenix vs. Los Angeles, October 9, 2002
On the night the Los Angeles Kings retired Wayne Gretzky's

No. 99, all did not go well for the Coyotes owner: he watched as his team become the first to be nailed for violating the NHL's new rule for speeding up play. The delay-of-game minor was called at 5:49 of the third period, as the Kings downed the Desert Dogs 4–1.

First game in which a penalized player returned to the ice after a power-play goal
Montreal vs. NHL All-Stars, October 9, 1956

Maurice Richard notched many historic goals, but his power-play marker at the 1956 All-Star game is rarely mentioned. After Richard scored, Red Sullivan of the All-Stars left the penalty box and skated back on the ice. This was an NHL first. Until the 1956–57 season, players served the full duration of their penalties, whether the opposing team scored with the man-advantage or not.

Last game in which two power-play goals were scored on the same minor penalty
Detroit vs. Montreal, April 10, 1956

During the last game of the 1956 finals, Jean Béliveau and Maurice Richard both beat Detroit goalie Glenn Hall while Marcel Pronovost was serving a minor for tripping. The two goals were the difference in Montreal's Cup-clinching 3–1 win.

First games using two referees
Detroit vs. Montreal, Boston vs. Toronto, Chicago vs. NY Americans, November 9, 1933

Sixty-five years before the NHL began experimenting with a two-referee, two-linesmen format in 1998–99, the league replaced the old referee-linesman setup with two referees, a head referee and an assistant referee. This arrangement lasted for several seasons, until the league settled on the familiar referee-and-two-linesmen system.

First game in which a goal judge was replaced due to incompetence
St. Louis vs. Colorado Rockies, April 1, 1979
It was no April Fool's joke. During the last game of the 1978–79 season, a wild 9–5 win for Colorado, goal judge Rod Lippman came down with a severe case of brain cramps. He failed to trigger his goal light after one goal, then later turned the light on twice when the puck hadn't even come close to entering the net. After the third mistake, referee Greg Madill ejected Lippman and had him replaced.

First game in which three assists were awarded on one goal
Detroit vs. Toronto, February 14, 1931
It was Valentine's Day, and the official scorer was in a giving mood. When Charlie Conacher scored, assists went to Joe Primeau, Busher Jackson and King Clancy. It was Toronto's lone goal in a 1–1 tie. (The NHL allowed a maximum of three assists on a goal for five seasons: from 1930–31 to 1935–36. It didn't happen often because forward passing was not allowed between zones.)

First game in which four assists were awarded on one goal
Toronto vs. NY Americans, January 10, 1935
A goal is scored, and all the players on the ice from the scoring team receive points? We're not sure how the official scorer got away with this one, but we do know that it happened. When Toronto's Joe Primeau scored on the power play at 13:52 of the

second period, assists were awarded to Charlie Conacher, Baldy
Cotton, Busher Jackson and Andy Blair.

First NHL game to draw 25,000 fans
Los Angeles vs. Pittsburgh, September 19, 1990
A record crowd of 25,581 attended an exhibition game between
Pittsburgh and Los Angeles at St. Petersburg's Suncoast Dome in
September 1990. The response encouraged the NHL to expand to
Florida two years later.

First hockey game to draw 70,000 fans
Michigan State vs. Michigan, October 6, 2001
The largest crowd ever assembled for a hockey game convened
at Spartan Stadium, where an artificial rink was set on the football field in front of 74,554 fans. The Michigan State Spartans
and Michigan Wolverines university hockey teams played to
a 3–3 tie. The game broke the previous attendance mark of
55,000, set on an outdoor rink in Moscow when the USSR hosted
Sweden at the 1957 World Championships.

First professional hockey games
The International Professional Hockey League, 1904
North America's first major pro league was founded by Michigan
dentist and hockey enthusiast J. L. Gibson. The league included
one team from Pittsburgh, three from Michigan (Houghton,
Calumet and Sault Ste. Marie) and one from the Canadian Soo.
Most of the players were Canadians. The IPHL folded after three
seasons, but the concept soon caught on.

First NHL game played in the United States
Montreal Maroons vs. Boston, December 1, 1924
Smokey Harris counted the game-winner when Boston won its

inaugural NHL game at the Boston Arena 2–1. It was not a sign of things to come: the Bruins proceeded to lose 11 straight.

First afternoon game
Detroit vs. Chicago, March 19, 1933
The Red Wings downed the Blackhawks 4–3 in the first NHL game contested during daylight.

First regular-season game played outside North America
Vancouver vs. Anaheim, Japan, October 4, 1997
The Canucks and the Mighty Ducks kicked off the 1997–98 season by playing a two-game series at Tokyo's Yoyogi Arena. The games were to help promote the participation of NHL players at the 1998 Winter Olympics in Nagano, Japan. The two teams split the series, trading 3–2 wins. Scott Walker of the Canucks made history by scoring the first goal in the first NHL match played outside North America.

First regular-season game played at a neutral site
Chicago vs. Pittsburgh Pirates, January 26, 1930
The struggling Pirates played several home games at neutral sites during the 1929–30 season. The first, a 5–2 loss to Chicago, was staged in New Jersey's Atlantic City. The next season, owner Benny Leonard moved the Pittsburgh franchise to Philadelphia and renamed his team the Quakers.

First regular-season game played a mile above sea level
Toronto vs. Colorado Rockies, October 5, 1976,
The first high-altitude NHL game took place in 1976, when the Colorado team, newly transferred from Kansas City, defeated Toronto 4–2 in its home opener at Denver's McNichols Sports Arena—5,280 feet above sea level.

First game played exclusively for British royalty

Chicago vs. Toronto, October 13, 1951

At 3 p.m., Chicago and Toronto played an abbreviated, one-period game at Maple Leaf Gardens—arranged for Princess Elizabeth and the Duke of Edinburgh. A few hours later, the same two teams took to the ice for the real season-opener, which Chicago won 3–1.

First game at which a queen dropped the puck
San Jose vs. Vancouver, October 6, 2002

In a royal first, Queen Elizabeth II dropped the ceremonial puck for a preseason game between the Vancouver Canucks and the San Jose Sharks. After completing her duties, the British monarch retired to a private box where she watched the first period with Wayne Gretzky. "She was curious about why penalties were called," said Gretzky. "She also talked about the goaltenders and how quick they were."

First NHL game attended by Babe Ruth

Chicago vs. Boston, November 15, 1927

Besieged by autograph hounds, the Bambino witnessed his first NHL game from rinkside at Boston Garden, as the Bruins hosted the Blackhawks. The contest was a rough one, featuring thundering checks, flailing elbows and a half-dozen fights. When a dazed Ruth made his way to an exit, he reportedly told a companion: "Never saw anything like it. Those fellows wanted to kill one another. Thank God I'm in baseball. It's so peaceful and quiet."

First NHL game attended by Gordie Howe's parents

Boston vs. Detroit, March 3, 1959

Howe's parents did not exactly rush out to see their son play in the big leagues. It was not until Gordie's 13th NHL season that Albert and Catherine Howe attended one of his games. The Saskatoon couple surprised their son by secretly arriving on Gordie Howe Night in the back seat of a new station wagon, which was wrapped in cellophane and wheeled on to the ice at the Detroit Olympia between the first and second periods of a game against Boston.

First U.S. president to attend an NHL game while in office
Bill Clinton, Washington, May 25, 1998
It wasn't until Clinton attended Game 2 of the 1998 Eastern Conference finals between the Capitals and the Buffalo Sabres (at Washington's MCI Center) that a sitting American president showed up at an NHL arena. Clinton, who watched the game from Capitals owner Abe Poulin's luxury suite, was impressed with the speed and fury. In a between-periods interview with ESPN, Clinton admitted that hockey was a much more exciting spectacle live than it was on TV.

Last game played at an Original Six arena
Chicago vs. Toronto, Maple Leafs Gardens, February 13, 1999
After 67 glorious years, the grand old lady of Carlton Street hosted her final NHL game. The visiting team was the Chicago Blackhawks, the same club that Toronto met in the first game played at the Gardens in 1931. The Hawks won that contest 2–1. This time, Chicago spoiled the party with a 6–2 triumph. Punch-out artist Bob Probert scored the last goal.

CHAPTER 2

Dollar
signs

In the summer of 1958, after
Montreal's third straight Stanley
Cup, Henri Richard took a job hawking oil, Doug
Harvey sold aluminum windows and Donnie
Marshall flogged beer. Those days are long gone.
In 1997–98, the NHL's average player salary topped
the U.S.$1-million mark for the first time. In
2002–03, it reached U.S.$1,750,000.

First player to sign a million-dollar contract

Bobby Orr, Boston, 1971

Ka-ching! The era of big-money hockey began with the Boston superstar, who inked a five-year $200,000-a-year contract with the Bruins prior to the 1971–72 season. Calculated over the duration of the deal, it made Orr the game's first million-dollar man.

First player to earn a million dollars in one season

Bobby Hull, Winnipeg Jets, 1972–73

Hull gave the World Hockey Association instant credibility when he signed a $2.75-million, 10-year contract with the Jets. The deal included a $1-million signing bonus, which made the Golden Jet an instant millionaire and opened the gates to spiralling salaries.

First player to screw up a million-dollar contract

Derek Sanderson, Philadelphia Blazers, 1972

A couple of weeks before Bobby Hull jumped to the WHA, Boston Bruins centre Derek Sanderson inked a five-year, U.S.$2.65-million contract with the Philadelphia Blazers. It reportedly made him the highest-paid athlete in North America—quite an upgrade considering Sanderson was making less than $15,000 a year with Boston. Unlike Hull's acquisition by the Winnipeg Jets, however, this deal was a bust; Sanderson never collected on his millions. Out of shape and disinterested, he played only eight games with Philadelphia before being injured. By the season's mid-point, Sanderson and the Blazers agreed to part company and he rejoined the Bruins.

Only player to agree to contracts with both an NHL and a WHA team—at the same time

Robert Picard, Washington and Quebec, 1977

On the day he was drafted in June 1977, Picard signed a letter of intent with the Washington Capitals. The first-round draft pick received a big bonus and spent some of it on a sports car. A couple of months later, the rookie defenseman signed a more lucrative five-year contract with the WHA's Quebec Nordiques. When the Caps protested, Picard declared: "I'd rather deliver pizzas in Quebec City than play for the Washington Capitals." After the Caps threatened a lawsuit, the WHA ruled Picard's contract with the Nordiques was invalid, and pizza boy reluctantly rejoined the Capitals.

First player to try and have his contract declared invalid—because he used a fax machine
Claude Lemieux, New Jersey, 1995

After the Devils won the Cup and Lemieux was voted MVP of the 1995 playoffs, the winger signed a new, three-year U.S.$4.1-million contract. A couple of months later, Lemieux decided he had made a mistake and should have held out for more money. He refused to report to camp, claiming his contract was invalid because he had faxed it back to the team. An arbitrator ruled in the Devils' favour. Lemieux was traded to Colorado before the season began.

First rookie to receive a multimillion-dollar contract
Alexandre Daigle, Ottawa, 1993–94

The Senators displayed somewhat less than sound judgment when they signed Daigle to a monstrous, five-year $12.25-million contract straight out of junior hockey. The deal sparked caustic comment around the league. Boston GM Harry Sinden said about Daigle: "He's fortunate we didn't have the first pick, because he's about $11.5 million richer than he would have been." Although Daigle netted 20 goals in his rookie season, he never developed into the star Ottawa had hoped for and was traded four years later. Daigle's signing was historically significant, however, as it led to the creation of a rookie salary cap in 1995.

First rookie with the potential to earn more than U.S.$8 million over the first three years of his contract

Rick Nash, Columbus, 2002

Nash's deal with the Blue Jackets is considered the richest rookie contract in NHL history, offering Nash a potential U.S.$8.56 million in performance bonuses alone during his first three years.

Only rookie to be the NHL's highest-paid player
Jean Béliveau, Montreal, 1953–54

Béliveau, who had been a huge star with the Quebec Aces of the Quebec Senior Hockey League, received $110,000 plus a slew of bonuses when he signed with Montreal in October 1953. He immediately became the NHL's highest-paid performer, making twice the salary of Gordie Howe and Maurice Richard.

First coach to receive a million-dollar contract

Jacques Demers, Detroit, June 1986

Detroit Red Wings owner Mike Ilitch opened the vault to land Demers, who had earned a reputation as a miracle worker in St. Louis. The five-year, U.S.$1.1-million deal was a huge upgrade from the $55,000 Demers had been making with the Blues, and it made him the highest-paid coach in NHL history. Demers revived the last-place Dead Things, who improved by 38 points to earn a berth in the Conference finals. He also guided Detroit to two Norris Division titles. But in 1990, when the Wings didn't win the Cup, Ilitch fired his high-priced saviour with a year left on his contract.

First big, front-loaded NHL contract

Keith Tkachuk, Winnipeg, 1995–95

In the summer of 1995, Tkachuk, a restricted free agent, signed a five-year, U.S.$17.2-million offer from the Chicago Blackhawks. Chicago made it tough for the small-market Jets to match the deal by front-loading the contract, giving Tkachuk U.S.$6 million in the first year. The Jets stubbornly signed Tkachuk, then stripped him of his captaincy. It was the death knell for the franchise, which fled to Phoenix the next season.

First player to receive a U.S.$15-million signing bonus

Joe Sakic, Colorado, 1996–97

The New York Rangers tried to obtain Sakic's services by dangling a three-year, U.S.$21-million offer sheet in front of the Group II free agent, including a humungous U.S.$15-million signing bonus. The Avalanche bit the bullet and matched the offer.

First player to earn more money in one season than another team's entire payroll

Sergei Fedorov, Detroit, 1997–98

In order to retain Fedorov, Detroit matched an exorbitant U.S.$28-million offer from the Carolina Hurricanes. The flashy forward cashed in big time with a U.S.$14-million signing bonus, U.S.$2 million in salary, plus a U.S.$12-million bonus if his team made the Conference finals. Fedorov made more than the Nashville Predators' entire U.S.$13.6-million payroll.

First player to sign a salary contract worth more than U.S.$10 million a year

Jaromir Jagr, Washington, 2001–02

Big money did not translate into big dividends for the Capitals. Jagr's offensive production took a sharp nosedive after the Czech winger signed a deal in the summer of 2001 that paid him a record-setting U.S.$10,033,333 per year.

First NHL salary cap
1925–26
The league's first salary cap was set at $35,000 for a 12-player team. The cap grew to $70,000 for a 14-man roster in 1932–33, with a provision that no player's salary could exceed $7,500. The cap was eliminated after the Depression ended in the late 1930s.

First year that a minimum NHL player salary was established
1958–59
The NHL set the minimum player's salary for the first time in 1958–59, at $7,000. The move was a reaction to the players' attempt to form a union the previous year. At the time, the minimum was about half of what most of the league's stars were earning. The minimum NHL salary in 2002–03 was U.S.$175,000, less than a fifth of what most stars make today.

First year that NHL player salaries were made public
1992
Soon after he assumed leadership of the NHLPA, in 1990, Bob Goodenow won an important victory for players by persuading NHL owners to agree to full salary disclosure. By setting public benchmarks for player salaries, it became easier for hockey agents to negotiate lucrative deals.

First NHL lockout
September 30, 1994
NHL owners shut down their arenas and locked out the players because there was no collective bargaining agreement in place.

The labour impasse lasted until January 20, 1995, when a new deal was signed. The NHL finished the season with an abbreviated 48-game schedule, the shortest since 1941–42.

First player to miss an entire year due to a contract dispute
Jake Forbes, Toronto St. Pats, 1921–22
Long before Alexei Yashin, there was goalie Jake Forbes, who stubbornly sat out the 1921–22 season in a contract dispute with the Toronto St. Pats. He was replaced by netminder John Ross Roach, who led Toronto to the Stanley Cup. Forbes lost a second chance to win the Cup as a member of the Hamilton Tigers in 1924–25, when his club was suspended for staging a strike during the playoffs. Forbes never did win the Cup.

First president of the NHL Players' Association
Ted Lindsay, Detroit, 1957
NHL owners were startled when Lindsay announced the formation of a players association in February 1957. But they quickly regrouped and set about destroying the fledgling organization. All of the association's key figures were either harassed or traded. Detroit GM Jack Adams dealt Lindsay to Chicago that summer, calling him "over the hill" even though the 33-year-old had just completed the best offensive season of his career, with 85 points in 70 games. Under pressure from the owners, and after gaining minor concessions from the league, the NHLPA disbanded within a year. It was not until 1967 that the NHLPA reformed, this time headed by lawyer Alan Eagleson.

First player to hire an agent
Carl Brewer, Toronto, 1963
In the fall of 1963, Brewer hired lawyer Alan Eagleson to help him negotiate a new contract with Toronto, a strategy unheard

of at the time. The move permanently soured the 25-year-old defenseman's already rocky relationship with coach Punch Imlach, and led to Brewer leaving the team two years later over another salary dispute. Ironically, it was Brewer's dogged investigation into the misuse of NHL Players' Association pension funds in the 1990s that led to Eagleson's downfall and public disgrace.

First free agent
Marcel Dionne, Detroit to Los Angeles, June 17, 1975
Dionne was the first player to fly the coop as a free agent. Without precedent, the NHL intervened and forced Los Angeles to trade Dan Maloney, Terry Harper and a second-round draft pick to the Red Wings as compensation.

First free agent signed without compensation
Bobby Orr, Boston to Chicago, June 24, 1976
No. 4's career in Boston ended when he signed a U.S.$3-million, five-year contract with the Blackhawks. The Bruins asked for no players in return, so hockey's most famous player changed teams without compensation, an NHL first. Orr's time in Chicago was brief. Unable to recover from knee miseries, he played only 26 games over two seasons before retiring.

First free-agent signing to cost a team five draft choices
Scott Stevens, Washington to St. Louis, July 16, 1990
Blues GM Ron Caron opened a new chapter in high-stakes free agency by signing Washington Capitals restricted free-agent defenseman Scott Stevens to a five-year, U.S.$5.1-million contract. According to the terms of the NHL's new collective-bargaining agreement, the Blues had to surrender five first-round draft choices to the Capitals as compensation.

First agent to find a performance-bonus loophole in the rookie salary cap
Mike Barnett, 1997

Joe Thornton's ground-breaking rookie contract in 1997 was engineered by Barnett, who turned the restrictive economics of salary caps in the entry-level system on their ear by taking advantage of the collective bargaining agreement's rookie bonuses for first-round picks. Barnett set a precedent whereby Thornton could cash in handsomely if he hit minimum standards in six categories, such as scoring, ice time and plus-minus spread, over his first three NHL seasons. This "ballooning" had real impact for Atlanta rookies Dany Heatley and Ilya Kovalchuk in 2001–02. They each made about U.S.$4 million in compensation.

First NHL star to sign a major endorsement deal
Gordie Howe, Detroit, 1960s

Howe's deal with TruLine equipment and sticks didn't make him rich, but it was an NHL first between a star and a national retailer (Eaton's).

First player from outside North America to sign an endorsement contract with a Fortune 500 company
Sergei Fedorov, Detroit, October 1995

The Russian centre inked a three-year deal with Nike to promote its new roller- and ice-hockey divisions. Fedorov and fellow-endorsers Brian Leetch and Scott Stevens gave the company its first shot of prime-time hockey exposure when they hit the ice at the 1996 All-Star game in Boston wearing Nike skates emblazoned with the Swoosh logo.

First player to lose half a million dollars betting on an Internet gambling site
Jaromir Jagr, Pittsburgh, 1998

In 2003, the NHL star admitted he had lost U.S.$500,000 wagering through an Internet gambling site, but insisted he paid the debt four years ago and did nothing illegal. "It was 1998, and I made mistakes," Jagr told reporters. "I wasn't smart. It was stupid." Jagr owed the cash to William Caesar, owner of the gambling website CaribSports, based in Belize. *Sports Illustrated* reported that Jagr agreed to pay U.S.$450,000—split into monthly payments—to settle the debt, and that Caesar leaked the story to the press after Jagr stopped making the payments. Caesar told *S.I.* that he had technicians configure Jagr's betting page so the hockey star could not bet on the NHL, which would be a violation of league rules. "We did that for our own protection, not just his," Caesar said. "That would destroy us, if he destroyed the game."

First NHL team to sign a joint-venture marketing deal with a Russian hockey club
Pittsburgh Penguins, February 1993

In 1993, an investment group led by Penguins owner Harold Baldwin bought a 50 per cent interest in the Moscow-based Central Red Army hockey club, and signed a management contract to run the club's arena. The aim was to provide the struggling Russian team with badly needed capital and NHL-style marketing, and to give the Penguins easier access to Russian players. The partnership lasted two years. By the spring of 1995, Russian criminals had taken control of the Central Army team, and when mobsters toting sawed-off shotguns under their leather trench coats began forcing out paying customers and claiming the arena's luxury suites for themselves, Baldwin and other Western sponsors pulled out.

First team publicly traded on the stock exchange
Florida Panthers, November 1996
Panthers owner Wayne Huizenga claimed to have lost U.S.$25 million on his hockey club in 1995, but he turned a losing venture into a profitable one in a single day in 1996, when he sold nearly six million shares of the Panthers (49 per cent of the team) for between U.S.$12 and $14 a share. Huizenga reaped U.S.$67.3 million for the club, which had been valued at U.S.$45 million by *Financial World* magazine.

First team to stage a strike
Hamilton Tigers, March 9, 1925
Money battles between owners and players are nothing new. After finishing first in the NHL in 1924–25, Hamilton Tigers players refused to compete in the playoffs until they were each paid a $200 bonus. The Tigers were upset because management had not boosted salaries when the league expanded from 24 to 30 games. When the players refused to budge, NHL president Frank Calder suspended the team and awarded the title to Montreal, which had defeated Toronto in a semifinal playoff series. Hamilton's franchise was sold, moved to New York and renamed the Americans.

First team to twice declare bankruptcy
Pittsburgh Penguins, 1975 and 1998
The Penguins first went into bankruptcy in June 1975, when owners Ted Potter and Peter Block folded under a U.S.$6.5-million debt. The NHL took over the team and sold it to Ohio businessman Al Savill. The Penguins filed for bankruptcy a

second time in October 1998, with owners Harold Baldwin and Roger Marino U.S.$100 million in the red. This filing led to Mario Lemieux taking over the team.

First team with a U.S.$70-million player payroll
New York Rangers, 2001–02
Manhattan has become synonymous with overpaid and under-achieving hockey teams. In 2001–02, the Rangers' payroll rose to a bloated U.S.$73 million. Despite the multimillion-dollar contracts paid to Mark Messier, Eric Lindros, Brian Leetch, Petr Nedved and others, New York missed the postseason for the fifth straight year.

Last team with a payroll under U.S.$20 million
Minnesota Wild, 2001–02
In its second season, the Wild spent a league-low U.S.$18.2 million, almost U.S.$4 million less than 29th-place Nashville's U.S.$22-million payroll. In 2002–03, salaries for all 30 NHL teams topped the U.S.$20-million mark, but Minnesota again got the biggest bang for its buck, spending U.S.$20.5 million.

Last team to win the Stanley Cup with a payroll in the NHL's bottom half
New Jersey Devils, 1999–2000
What price victory? New Jersey is the only club since 1990 to win the Cup with a payroll that sits in the NHL's lower parliament. The Devils' U.S.$31.3-million payout ranked 15th in a league of 28 teams in 1999–2000.

CHAPTER 3

Tools
of the trade

Today's hockey equipment is

lighter, more protective and, in

the case of goalies, fatter. During the 1990s, this

oversized equipment prompted the NHL to

appoint its first inspector, Dave Dryden, to weed

out illegal goalie gear. Meanwhile, technology

has produced composite sticks that add 10 to

20 m.p.h. to players' shots.

First NHL puck enscribed with a hockey personality's name
The Art Ross puck, 1940–41
Art Ross's influence on the game both as a coach and inventor should not be underestimated. He designed the NHL's B-shaped goal net, and refined the design of the puck so it would slide more smoothly and be easier to manufacture. In 1940–41, the Art Ross puck (adorned with an orange label bearing its designer's name) became the official puck of the NHL. As Ross's son once observed: "The object of hockey is to put the Art Ross puck in the Art Ross net and win the Art Ross Trophy."

First NHL player to use a curved stick
Andy Bathgate, NY Rangers, late 1950s
Although Chicago's Stan Mikita and Bobby Hull popularized the curved stick in the mid-1960s, hockey historians agree that Bathgate was the first to use a bent blade on a consistent basis. He began experimenting with curving his sticks as a youth and refined the technique after he turned pro. As Bathgate once told an interviewer: "I would heat up the blades with hot water, then I could bend them. I would put them in the toilet-stall door jam and leave them overnight. The next day they would have a hook in them." To stop the sticks from straightening out, Bathgate added fibreglass to his blades—another hockey first.

First NHL goalie to use a curved stick
Ron Hextall, Philadelphia, 1986–87
Hextall is regarded as one of the great goalie puck handlers. Long before he joined the NHL, he was working on his shot. He began using a curved stick before any other netminder, optimizing his puckhandling and passing to act as a third defenseman on dump-ins.

First player to use an aluminum-shafted stick

Brad Park, Detroit, early 1980s

Park used an Easton-built graphite compound stick at practice for 18 months before the NHL allowed it in games. He championed the new technology and reported to the *Hockey News:* "You have a stick that has the same weight all the time, the same stiffness, the same feel. And on top of that, it's less expensive." Well, three out of four ain't bad: Park was right about everything except the money.

First NHL player to wear a helmet

George Owen, Boston, 1929

A former college hockey star, Owen debuted with the Bruins on January 10, 1929. A native of Hamilton, Ontario, he also played football at university, and reportedly wore his leather football helmet as a rookie blueliner in the NHL. Owen went on to win the Cup with Boston in 1929.

Last NHL player to skate without a helmet

Craig MacTavish, St. Louis, 1996–97

Helmets were rare until the early 1970s. As a result, a lot of players were known for their long hair (Derek Sanderson, Ron Duguay)—or lack of (Bill White, Gary Bergman). That all began to change in 1979, when the NHL made helmets mandatory for all players entering the league; for anyone already in the NHL, they were voluntary. MacTavish, the last of the bareheaded breed, played his final game for the Blues during the 1997 playoffs.

First NHL team on which all players wore helmets

Boston Bruins, January 4, 1934

The Bruins must have been riding a roller coaster of emotions after defenseman Eddie Shore laid out Toronto's Ace Bailey

December 12, 1933, with a crushing body check that hospitalized the star Maple Leaf. Bailey hovered near death for several days with a fractured skull. Shore was suspended indefinitely, and, as American newspapers ripped the sport for its violence, attendance dropped by the thousands at Boston Garden. In Ottawa, for the first time the entire team donned leather helmets to play the Senators. The Bruins were whipped 9–2.

First use of computerized hockey helmets
NHL All-Star game, February 4, 2001
Hockey jumped into the future when Ray Bourque, Pavel Bure, Theo Fleury and Nicklas Lidstrom donned helmets outfitted with miniature circuit boards at the 2001 All-Star game. The units emitted radio signals, which were relayed to technicians in a control truck to record how fast, how far and where each player skated. The technology, developed by Massachusetts' Trakus Inc., may soon become a regular component of hockey telecasts. Bourque registered the fastest speed (22.9 m.p.h.), while Fleury skated the farthest (2.8 miles).

First goalie to wear a mask
Clint Benedict, Montreal Maroons, January 1930
The distinction of being the first masked netminder falls to Benedict, who tried a crude leather model for a couple of games after suffering a broken cheekbone. He gave it up because it obscured his vision on low shots.

First goalie to regularly wear a mask
Jacques Plante, Montreal, 1959–60
Plante put a new face on hockey during a 3–1 Montreal win against the New York Rangers on November 1, 1959. After an Andy Bathgate shot shredded his nose, Plante donned his home-

made fibreglass mask for the first time. Today, it is considered a goalie's most important piece of equipment.

Last NHL goalie to play without a mask
Andy Brown, Pittsburgh, April 7, 1974
Brown was the last of the barefaced goalies. His final NHL game was a 6–3 Penguins loss to the Atlanta Flames. He went on to play three years in the WHA and never wore a mask in that league either. The journeyman netminder was a feisty character. In 1973–74 with the Penguins, he set a single-season NHL record for goalkeepers with 60 penalty minutes. The next year, with the WHA Indianapolis Racers, Brown led all goalies with 75 PIM, the second-highest total on his team.

First goalie to decorate his mask
Gerry Cheevers, Boston, 1967–68
Cheevers first painted his mask with black stitch-marks as a joke, after a shot by Fred Stanfield at practice scratched his face protector. The zipper-like motif inspired a trend of self-expression as other goalies began to decorate their masks with team logos and more stylized designs.

First goalie to have his mask stolen during a game
Bernie Parent, Toronto, April 8, 1971
The Leafs were leading the Rangers 4–1 in this 1971 playoff tilt when a brawl broke out in the third period. During the mêlée, Rangers winger Vic Hadfield tore off Parent's mask and tossed it into the stands. When the public-address announcer requested its return, the fans at Madison Square Garden chanted, "Don't give it back! Don't give it back!" The mask was not returned, and

Parent, who didn't have another mask on hand, had to give way to backup Jacques Plante. A few days later, Parent's mask was mailed to him, with no explanation enclosed.

First goalie to use a blocker
Frank Brimsek, Boston, 1940s

There is no exact date for when Brimsek wore the NHL's first blocker, but that model certainly wouldn't be up to today's bulletproof standards. To stop shots with the back of his right hand, Brimsek built bamboo ribbing into his stick-glove.

First goalie to wear a trapper's glove
Emile Francis, Chicago, 1947–48

It wasn't until the late 1940s that the NHL netminding brigade could boast a suitable catching glove. Until then, goalies wore a regular hockey glove with a piece of leather sewn between the thumb and the forefinger of their catching hand. Francis took a three-fingered first baseman's mitt and sewed on a protective cuff. His hybrid creation became hockey's first trapper.

First goalies to be caught wearing illegal-sized leg pads
Sam LoPresti, Chicago, 1941–42
Earl Robertson, Brooklyn Americans, 1941–42

Goalies used to bang their pads with their sticks to flatten the fronts, making them slightly wider than regulation size. In this 1941–42 game, Americans coach Red Dutton asked for a measurement of Chicago goalie Sam LoPresti's pads. Referee Bill Chadwick ruled they were $10\frac{1}{4}$ inches—one-quarter-inch wider than the legal limit. Irate Chicago coach Paul Thompson immediately requested a measurement of the pads worn by Brooklyn's Earl Robertson. To Dutton's chagrin, they measured $10\frac{1}{4}$ inches. But because there was no penalty in the rule book for wearing illegal pads, Chadwick let the game continue. The next year, a minor penalty was assessed for illegal pads.

First NHL goalies to put a water bottle on the net
Pelle Lindbergh and Bob Froese, Philadelphia, 1984–85
Today, all NHL netminders keep fluids close at hand, thanks to Lindbergh and Froese, who likely got the idea from U.S. college goalies. Still, when they introduced the practice, some thought it a sissified idea. Smarting after a 4–1 loss to the Flyers in Game 1 of the 1985 Cup finals, Edmonton Oilers coach Glen Sather sneered, "What are they going to want up there next, a bucket of chicken?" At Sather's insistence, Lindbergh's water bottle was removed, and the Oilers went on to win the Cup.

First goalie to wear No. 0
Paul Bibeault, Montreal, 1942–43
Bibeault just couldn't make up his mind. He also wore No. 1, 14, 16 and 21 during his 102-game career with Montreal.

First non-goalie to wear No. 0
Neal Sheehy, Hartford, 1987–88
Sheehy wore No. 0 for 26 games, while playing defense in Hartford. As he once confessed: "Zero is the furthest number from 99, and, talent-wise, I was as far away from 99 as possible. But remember, opposites attract." He also said, "When my grand-parents came to the U.S. from Ireland, our family name was O'Sheehy. I wore No. 0 to get the 'O' back."

First goalie to wear No. 00
Bernie Parent, Philadelphia Blazers, 1972–73
John Davidson of the Rangers donned double zero in 1975–76 because teammates Phil Esposito and Ken Hodge were wearing

No. 77 and No. 88, respectively. But Davidson was beaten to the punch by Bernie Parent, who wore No. 00 for one season with the WHA Philadelphia Blazers. Asked why he chose those numerals, Parent replied: "Every time a puck gets past me and I look back in the net, I say, 'Oh, oh!'"

Last goalie to wear No. 00
Martin Biron, Buffalo, 1995–96
Biron wore No. 00 during a three-game stint with the Sabres in 1995–96. By the time he got another start for Buffalo, three years later, the NHL had passed a rule banning the number. Biron now wears No. 43.

First pro player to wear a decimal number
Roydun Gunn, Memphis River Kings, 1993–94
As a play on his name, Gunn, and the .45-calibre revolver, the Saskatchewan-born goalie wore the decimal .45 in 1993–94 with the Central Hockey League's Memphis River Kings. Gunn's sweater now hangs in the Hockey Hall of Fame.

First pro player to wear a triple-digit number
Mel Hewitt, IHL Salt Lake Golden Eagles, 1986–87
Hewitt must have had a good reason for wearing No. 111. It certainly made him stand out. He also wore No. 19 that season.

First three-digit number retired by a team
739, NY Islanders, 1997
Coaches don't wear numbers, so the Islanders found another way to honour Al Arbour. On January 25, 1997, they raised a banner with the number 739 to the rafters of Nassau Coliseum, to commemorate the 739 regular-season wins Arbour racked up behind the Islanders' bench.

Firsts: retired uniform numbers

FIRST RETIRED NO.	PLAYER	NUMBER	TEAM	DATE
Of a player	Ace Bailey	No. 6	Toronto	02/14/1934
Of a D-man	Lionel Hitchman	No. 3	Boston	mid-1930s
Of a goalie	Bernie Parent	No. 1	Phil	10/11/1979
Of an American	Rod Langway	No. 5	Washington	11/26/1997
Of a European	Stan Mikita	No. 21	Chicago	10/19/1980
Of a Euro-trainee	Thomas Steen	No. 25	Winnipeg	05/06/1995

First team to put numbers on the front of its uniforms

Boston Bruins, 1936–37

Boston is the only NHL team to feature numbers on both the back and front of its jerseys for an extended period of time. The club stuck with this uninspiring concept for 12 years before introducing its familiar spoked-B crest.

First team to put player names on its uniforms

New York Americans, 1925–26

In their first NHL season, the Americans put player names on the backs of their flashy, star-spangled red-white-and-blue jerseys, a first in pro sports and an innovation the NHL did not make mandatory until the 1970s.

Last team to put player names on its uniforms

Toronto Maple Leafs, 1978–79

In February 1978, the NHL passed a rule that teams must put their players' names on the backs of both home and road jerseys. But tight-fisted Toronto owner Harold Ballard did not want to put names on the Leafs' home attire—he felt it would hurt program sales. Ballard was able to resist the change until the following season, due to a contract with the manufacturer of the Leafs' program that stipulated no names on the backs of home jerseys in 1977–78.

First team to put a corporate emblem on its crest
Vancouver Canucks, 1997–98
In the language of corporate-speak, they call this synergy. The Canucks adopted new uniforms in 1997–98 bearing a killer-whale crest—picked because the marine mammal is a powerful north-west aboriginal symbol. However, a killer whale also happens to be the corporate logo of Orca Bay Sports and Entertainment, the company that owns the Canucks.

Only team to replace its crest with a globe, representing Earth
Montreal Canadiens, 1924–25
The globe replaced the traditional CH crest for one season, because, after winning the 1924 Stanley Cup, Montreal wanted to remind everyone that it was the best hockey team in the world.

First team to put a woman's image on its crest
New York Rangers, 1996–97
The Rangers' third jersey features the crowned visage of Lady Liberty above the letters NYR. The idea of using the famed land-mark came from Rangers GM Neil Smith: "We wanted a look that was identifiable with New York, and the Statue of Liberty was a better choice than, say, the Empire State Building."

First appearance of the CH crest on Montreal's uniform
1916–17
Sacre bleu! Not only did the Canadiens' early sweaters not have the popular CH crest, in 1910–11, Montreal's red sweaters sported

a green maple-leaf emblem. It wasn't until 1916 that the Canadiens' famous emblem—a large "C" surrounding a small "H"—was adopted.

First appearance of the maple leaf crest on Toronto's uniform
1927–28

Canada's national symbol was first affixed to the front of Toronto's sweaters in 1927–28, the season that super-patriot Conn Smythe became owner. At the time, the team was known as the St. Pats, and the players wore green uniforms. Smythe changed all that, making the colour scheme true blue.

First teams to wear a third jersey
Pittsburgh, Boston, Vancouver, Los Angeles, Anaheim, January 1996

Seeking to boost revenues through merchandise sales, the NHL announced that five teams would don newly designed third jerseys January 27, 1996. The so-called "fashionable authentic" jerseys were worn at selected home games for the rest of the season. Of the five clubs, only Pittsburgh and Boston continued to wear their third jerseys on a regular basis. The Canucks, Kings and Mighty Ducks soon scrapped their outfits—a move widely applauded. The Kings and Mighty Ducks' duds were among the ugliest seen on NHL ice.

Only team to wear white skates
California Golden Seals, 1971–72

After buying California's franchise in 1970, flamboyant owner Charles Finley changed the Seals' uniforms to green and gold and put player names on the back. The next year, he had the

Seals' skates painted white to match the shoes worn by his baseball team, the Oakland Athletics. The skates had to be repeatedly painted to cover up scuff marks; by the end of the year, the players swore they weighed 20 pounds.

Only team to wear white pants
Washington Capitals, 1974–75
Not all new ideas are good ones. For the first month of their inaugural season, the Capitals wore albino pants with red jerseys for road games. The pants didn't impress anyone (much like Washington's team), and had the added disadvantage of turning transparent when the players sweated. The white pants were soon replaced with blue ones.

First team to wear long pants
Philadelphia Flyers, 1981–82
The Flyers wanted to do more than make a radical fashion state-ment when they adopted long pants in 1981–82. The idea was to create a faster, more streamlined uniform with lighter, slimmer padding. Whether the long pants made the Flyers players skate faster is debatable, but they definitely made them slide faster into the boards. After the Hartford Whalers copied the innova-tion in 1982–83, the NHL banned long pants.

CHAPTER 4

Smells
like
team spirit

Before the Blues, St. Louis had the

Eagles; and before the Penguins,

Pittsburgh had the Pirates. The first team to return

to a city with the same name is Ottawa, whose

Senators were reborn in 1992. Today, Ottawa is

again threatened by the financial woes that killed

the original Senators in 1934. Same city, same name,

same story.

First organized hockey team
McGill University, Montreal
The birthplace of hockey may be in dispute, but most historians
concur that McGill students formed the first organized team.
Using codified rules, hockey officials and team uniforms, the
McGill team played a three-game series in February 1877 against
an informal squad of lacrosse and football players called the
Victorias. McGill won the series 2–1.

First NHL team to relocate
Quebec Bulldogs, 1920
There is nothing new about NHL teams changing cities. In
1920, after only one season in the league, the last-place Quebec
Bulldogs and their scoring champion Joe Malone were bought
by Hamilton businessmen and moved to Steeltown, where they
were renamed the Tigers.

First NHL city to wait 60 years between NHL games
Hamilton, Ontario
Hamilton's NHL franchise had completed just five seasons when
the club was moved to New York, after its final home game
March 7, 1925. Hamilton waited 67 years before the NHL returned,
for a neutral-site game October 20, 1992, with Toronto beating
Ottawa 5–3. Quebec City suffered a 59-year wait, from 1920 when
the Bulldogs folded to 1979's arrival of the Nordiques. Ottawa suffered a similar 58-year stretch of absenteeism, from 1934 to 1992.

First American-based NHL team
Boston Bruins, 1924–25
The Bruins joined the NHL due to the efforts of department store
magnate Charles Adams, who anted up $15,000 for an NHL fran-
chise in 1924. Boston struggled in its first two seasons, but vaulted

into the ranks of the league's elite in 1926–27 after acquiring Eddie Shore from the defunct Western Canada Hockey League.

First team to open a new arena with a riot
Boston Bruins, November 20, 1928

The opening of brand-new Boston Garden was supposed to get Bruins supporters excited, but not this excited. By game time, there were 17,000 fans jammed into the arena (3,500 more than capacity), with hundreds of late arrivals clamouring to get in. Fights broke out between police and the surging crowd outside. As the riot raged, the Canadiens blanked the Bruins 1–0.

First team to average 20,000 fans per game, one season
Chicago Blackhawks, 1994–95

During 24 home games in 1994–95's abbreviated season, the Blackhawks averaged 20,810 fans at the new United Center, up from 17,776 in their final season at Chicago Stadium.

First team to draw 25,000 fans, one game
Tampa Bay Lightning, October 9, 1993

The Lightning drew an NHL-record 27,227 spectators for its 1993 home opener against the Florida Panthers. The Suncoast Dome had a 28,000 seating capacity for hockey games, and the Lightning averaged 19,656 fans per game in 1993–94.

Only team to play home games on the road to boost attendance
Chicago Blackhawks, 1954–55

How bad must things be when you have to go on the road to draw a decent crowd? Chicago played eight home games at neutral sites in 1954–55, and discovered it could draw larger audiences playing away than at Chicago Stadium, where disgruntled fans had lost interest in a team that had finished last in five of seven seasons. The Blackhawks played six games in St. Louis, Missouri; one each in Omaha, Nebraska, and St. Paul, Minnesota. Some things never change, though. Chicago won only one of eight neutral-site games.

First NHL team to play a game inside a prison
Detroit Red Wings, February 2, 1954

In one of the strangest hockey games ever staged, Gordie Howe, Ted Lindsay and the rest of the first-place Red Wings met the Marquette Prison Pirates, a club composed of murderers, arsonists and bank robbers from one of America's toughest prisons. The match was arranged because Detroit GM Jack Adams was a friend of Leonard "Oakie" Brumm, the Marquette Prison's athletic director. The entire penitentiary population of 600 attended the afternoon tilt. At the post-game banquet, the Michigan cons presented Adams with a "honey bucket," the prison's version of a maximum-security toilet. Adams declared: "This is a great day. I'm proud to have such a fine 'farm' team up here in the north. The only trouble is, you guys have made it tough for me to recruit any of you."

First team saddled with a curse
Chicago Blackhawks, 1927

According to legend, the Blackhawks' first coach, Pete Muldoon, placed a hex on the team after he was fired at the end of the 1926–27 season. Muldoon vowed the Hawks would never finish first. Four decades passed before Chicago broke the "curse," in 1966–67. As the Hawks celebrated their league title, Stan Mikita quipped, "Is the champagne cold? It should be. It's been on ice for 40 years." (Toronto sportswriter Jim Coleman later admitted he invented the hex story when faced with a pressing deadline.)

First team to hire a hypnotist
New York Rangers, 1950–51
Mired in a 12-game losing streak, Rangers coach Neil Colville hired a hypnotist to instil a jolt of confidence. On November 15, 1950, Dr. David Tracy put the Rangers under his spell before a game with the Boston Bruins. But Tracy's efforts went for nought: the mesmerized Blueshirts blew a lead and lost 4–3. The doctor was not invited back.

First team to use a magic elixir
New York Rangers, 1950–51
A month after their failed hypnotist experiment, the Rangers found a new gimmick: a supposedly energizing drink cooked up by restaurant owner Gene Leone. Several players began drinking the miracle brew before games, and, when the team started winning, its popularity spread. The potion's appeal lasted as long as the Rangers' on-ice success, which was not long. By the end of the year, the Blueshirts had dropped to fifth place and Leone's magic elixir was down the drain.

First team to use a hyperbaric oxygen chamber
Vancouver Canucks, 1993–94
During Vancouver's run to the 1994 finals, its players spent a lot of time sitting inside a metal capsule with an oxygen mask clamped over their mouths. The oxygen-rich hyperbaric chamber had long been used to treat burn victims and divers suffering from the bends, but in 1993–94, the Canucks became the first pro team in North America to use it to treat injuries. Although the hyperbaric chamber ultimately proved more a product of

stock-market hype than substance, that didn't stop the Canucks from swearing to its healing powers. During the playoffs, the team used the chamber on a regular basis, not only to treat injuries but to combat jet lag.

First team to employ a costumed mascot
Quebec Nordiques, 1983
The Nordiques mascot was a fuzzy, roly-poly blue creature known as Badaboum, who entertained fans at the Quebec Colisée with his freaky dance routines. Badaboum vanished into history—along with the Nords—in 1995.

First team to play a game against circus bears
Edmonton Oilers, 1988
How far the mighty had fallen. A decade after their great dynasty run, the Oilers were trying to drum up flagging fan interest with animal acts. In December 1998, Edmonton had three of its Russian players—Mikhail Shtalenkov, Andrei Kovalenko and Boris Mironov—play a little three-on-three hockey with a troika of bears from a visiting Russian circus. Wrote Alan Maki of the *Globe and Mail:* "The bears, who wore skates and helmets and looked about as mobile as Vancouver Canucks defenseman Dana Murzyn, took on the Oilers trio and were beaten like a rug."

Only team named after a children's movie
Anaheim Mighty Ducks, 1993
At the news conference to announce Anaheim's entry into the NHL March 1, 1993, team president Michael Eisner, Los Angeles Kings owner Bruce McNall and NHL commissioner Gary Bettman tooted duck calls in unison. The comic touch was fitting. Eisner, the CEO of the Disney Corporation, had defied the critics and

named his new NHL team after a Disney children's movie, *The Mighty Ducks*. Although many felt the name was lame, Eisner reasoned the moniker would lend his club instant brand-name recognition. He also figured it would boost ticket sales for the *Mighty Ducks* sequel, released in 1994.

First team to fly to an NHL game
New York Rangers, 1929

Although air travel wouldn't become a common mode of transport for NHL teams until the 1960s, the Rangers took to the skies three decades earlier. In 1929, club president Colonel John Hammond hired the Curtis-Wright Corporation to fly his team to Toronto for a game. Hammond was clearly not a superstitious man. The flight departed Friday the 13th. But flying didn't help the Blueshirts; they lost 7–6.

First NHL teams to play exhibition games in Europe
Montreal Canadiens and Detroit Red Wings, 1938

At the end of the 1937–38 season, Montreal and Detroit departed for Europe by steamship to play a nine-game exhibition tour in England and France. The first contest was played in London before a crowd of 8,000. Montreal won 5–4 on an overtime goal by Toe Blake.

Only NHL teams to play an extended European exhibition tour
New York Rangers and Boston Bruins, 1959

Bizarre, but true. The Rangers and Bruins conducted a 23-stop tour through Europe in the spring of 1959, playing in Paris, Vienna and other major cities. New York added Bobby Hull to its roster for the series, and the Golden Jet played on a line with Eddie Shack—a pairing that must have been an amazing sight.

First team associated with the term "firewagon hockey"

Montreal Canadiens, 1950s

During the Canadiens' glory years of the 1950s, the phrase "firewagon hockey" was coined to describe the high-speed, razzle-dazzle style of game played by Maurice Richard, Jean Béliveau and company. The expression was synonymous with the Montreal style for two decades.

First team associated with the term "goon hockey"

Philadelphia Flyers, mid-1970s

The Flyers' transformation from being a team of 98-pound weaklings to being a gang of Visigoths began in the 1969 play-offs, when they were physically abused by the St. Louis Blues and eliminated in four straight games. Embarrassed owner Ed Snider vowed to toughen them up. Three years later, the bulked-up Flyers were known as the Broad Street Bullies. Led by Dave "The Hammer" Schultz, Bob "Houndog" Kelly and Andre "Moose" Dupont, Philly embarked on an unprecedented reign of violence—and won two Stanley Cups.

First team accused of being a "cult"

Minnesota Wild, 2002–03

"The Minnesota Wild is not a hockey team. It is a cult," declared Vancouver Canucks GM Brian Burke prior to his team's playoff series with Minnesota in April 2003. Burke wasn't accusing the Wild of being devil worshippers. He was alluding to the team's single-minded devotion to coach Jacques Lemaire's teachings. As Burke noted: "They've got total buy-in on their system." Minnesota's defense-first philosophy served it well in the 2003 playoffs, as the club rallied twice from three-games-to-one deficits to upset the Colorado Avalanche and Burke's Canucks.

First team to unofficially ban high uniform numbers
Ottawa Senators, 1997–98

Under autocrat GM Pierre Gauthier, the Senators flushed more than Alexandre Daigle when they dealt their high-priced, under-achieving number one draft pick in January 1998. By ridding the club of Daigle and his No. 91 jersey, Gauthier figured the long-suffering franchise had turned the corner. To make it work he forced everyone to wear numbers in the lower stratosphere, believing that a few players with higher digits would affect team unity. For his part, Daigle tried reversing his own fortunes with his new team, the Philadelphia Flyers. He wore No. 19.

First team to trade a player to two different teams at the same time
Quebec Nordiques, 1992

The pressure of what to do with Eric "I won't play in Quebec City" Lindros finally got to Nordiques president Marcel Aubut. In June 1992, he traded Lindros to the Philadelphia Flyers. Then, before the hour was out, he impulsively struck another deal to send Lindros to the New York Rangers. The NHL had to hire an arbitrator to sort out the mess. He decided the first deal was valid, and Lindros went to Philadelphia. But the deal still proved a winner for Quebec, when the club landed budding superstar Peter Forsberg. (Although the benefits were short-lived. Quebec's franchise moved to Colorado in 1995.)

First team to feature three brothers on one line
Chicago Blackhawks, 1942–43

During the 1940s, centre Max Bentley and left-winger Doug Bentley formed one of the NHL's most lethal offensive duos.

Then, on January 1, 1943, Chicago coach Paul Thompson called Reg Bentley up from the minors and inserted him on right wing—alongside his two younger siblings—in a game against the New York Rangers. In a return match two nights later in New York, all three brothers recorded points in a 3–3 game. It was the first time in NHL annals that three brothers skated as linemates, a feat not duplicated until 1981, when Peter, Marian and Anton Stastny played as a unit with the Quebec Nordiques.

First team to ice a five-man Russian unit
Detroit Red Wings, 1995–96
In a radical departure from conventional thinking at the time, Red Wings coach Scotty Bowman put together an all-Russian five-man unit composed of forwards Sergei Fedorov, Igor Larionov and Slava Kozlov, with Slava Fetisov and Vladimir Konstantinov on defense. The puckhandling skills of the Soviet-trained quintet helped the high-flying Wings set a new NHL record of 62 wins.

First team to rotate captains on a regular basis
Minnesota Wild, 2000–01
In its first NHL season, the Wild appointed a new captain each month from October to April as a reward for outstanding play. The idea came from coach Jacques Lemaire, who declared: "We will try to give every player a chance to show his leadership to this hockey club." Defenseman Brad Bombardir was the first repeat captain, earning the "C" in January and February.

CHAPTER 5

Northern
lights

When Jordin Tootoo was chosen

98th overall by Nashville in 2001, he

became the first Inuit player drafted into the NHL.

Growing up near the Arctic Circle in the remote

village of Rankin Inlet, he didn't play organized

hockey until age 14. Tootoo is also the first NHL

prospect with a harpoon scar on his hand (which

he picked up while seal hunting).

First NHL superstar
Howie Morenz, 1923–24 to 1936–37

Morenz was without peer as hockey's most colourful and popular player during the NHL's early years. His end-to-end rushes were breathtaking, his box office appeal unparalleled while he brought new fans to the game and helped popularize the sport in America. In his 14-year career with the Canadiens, Blackhawks and Rangers, he won numerous MVP awards, scoring titles and three Stanley Cups. Known as the "Babe Ruth of Hockey," Morenz recorded 472 points in 550 games.

First elite NHL goaltenders
Georges Vezina, 1917–18 to 1925–26
Clint Benedict, 1917–18 to 1929–30

The first goaltenders of any prominence were Vezina and Benedict. Vezina, the stalwart Montreal Canadiens backstopper whose legacy is perpetuated with a goaltending trophy, never missed a match in 15 years of playing for the NHA and NHL. His 327-game streak includes two Stanley Cups and eventual induction as the first goalie in the Hall of Fame. Benedict, less well-remembered, pioneered several changes, including the rule that allowed goalies to drop to the ice. He was a master at forcing stoppages in play and playing hurt. "Getting hurt was nothing," Benedict once said. "I've been hit so hard (by the puck) that it bounced off my head and into the seats. They stitched me up and put me back in." Benedict won four Cups and had better goal averages and shutout totals than Vezina, but waited until 1965 for his Hall of Fame notice.

First European-trained NHL star
Borje Salming, 1973–74 to 1989–90

A frequent target of taunts and physical abuse, Salming was

point man for the European invasion of the NHL. He helped dispel the "chicken Swede" mindset in the largely Canadian league and developed into an elite defenseman, blocking shots, leading the rush and setting up plays with Toronto (and Detroit for one season) during a 17-year career. He was named an NHL All-Star for six straight years and joined the Hall of Fame in 1996.

First full-blooded aboriginal NHL player
Fred Saskamoose, Chicago, 1953–54

Saskamoose, a Cree from Saskatchewan's Sandy Lake Reserve, skated in 11 games with Chicago, recording no points and six penalty minutes in his brief big-league stint. He later served as playing coach of the Kamloops Chiefs, where the Shushwap and Chilcotin Bands of the B.C. interior proclaimed him Chief Thunder Stick, an honourary title he adopted when he was elected chief of the Sandy Lake Crees.

First black NHL player
Willie O'Ree, Boston, 1957–58, 1960–61

O'Ree's pro hockey career stretched from 1956 to 1979, but he played only 45 NHL games. A victim of racial abuse, both from opposing players and fans (who insulted him by throwing black hats onto the ice), he skated in his first match January 18, 1958, on a line with Boston's Don McKenney and Jerry Toppazzini. O'Ree scored only 14 points during his brief NHL career, but was one of the best and most popular players in the Western Hockey League between 1962 and 1974. O'Ree was born in Fredericton, New Brunswick.

First woman to play in the NHL

Manon Rheaume, Tampa Bay, 1992–93

Rheaume played one period of preseason hockey in the nets against St. Louis on September 23, 1992. She allowed two goals on nine shots in the publicity stunt.

First Hispanic NHL player

Scott Gomez, New Jersey, 1999–2000

Gomez, the first Mexican-American NHLer, notched a Calder-winning performance in his 70-point rookie season, 1999–2000. Remarking on his Latino status, he said, "It's not like I'm breaking any barriers, not like Jackie Robinson."

First NHL player of Asian ancestry

Larry Kwong, NY Rangers, March 13, 1948

Kwong, the son of a Chinese grocer in B.C., got one crack at the NHL, and it lasted just one shift; but long enough for this NHL first.

First Finnish-born player

Albert Pudas, Toronto St. Pats, 1926–27

A native of Siikajoki, Finland, Pudas played his formative hockey years in Port Arthur, Ontario, before his brief four-game stint with Toronto in 1926–27. For some reason Port Arthur was a hotbed of Finnish nationals. The second Finn in NHL action, Pentti Lund, also played in Port Arthur. He later won the Calder Trophy as rookie of the year, with the Rangers in 1948–49.

First Swedish-born player

Gustav Forslund, Ottawa, 1932–33

Another Nordic native who grew up in Ontario's Port Arthur-Fort William area (now Thunder Bay), Forslund scored 13 points in the 48-game 1932–33 season. He was born in Umea, Sweden.

First Czech-born player
Stan Mikita, Chicago, 1958–59 to 1979–80

A household name during the four decades of his career, Mikita emigrated to Canada in 1948 from Sokolce, Czechoslovakia, at age 8, with his aunt and uncle. He settled in St. Catherines, Ontario. Mikita scored 1,467 points in 1,394 games.

First Russian-born player
Val Hoffinger, Chicago, 1927–28 to 1928–29

Chicago's Johnny Gottselig is often erroneously cited as the first Russian to skate in the NHL. That might be because his career included two Stanley Cups. In fact, little-known defenseman Val Hoffinger, a native of Seltz, Russia, beat Gottselig by one season; he joined the NHL in 1927–28. Hoffinger played just 28 games; Gottselig, 589.

First Russian-trained player
Viktor Nechaev, Los Angeles, 1982–83

Picked 132nd overall by the Kings in the 1982 entry draft, Nechaev emigrated to the U.S. after marrying an American nurse he met in Russia. The Soviet Union's first NHLer played just three games and posted one point before being demoted to the minors.

First player to defect from the Soviet Union
Alexander Mogilny, Central Red Army, 1989

Considered the future of Russian hockey, a 20-year-old Mogilny bolted from the USSR at the 1989 World Championships in Sweden. He signed with representatives of the Buffalo Sabres in Stockholm. His defection, after years of military service with the

Central Red Army, caused a political fire-storm. Mogilny's alienation from his homeland was still evident in 2002, when he refused to represent his country at the Olympics.

First former NHLer to play in Russia
Vincent Riendeau, 1998–99
After Riendeau's NHL career ended in 1995, he took his pads on the road, tending net in Italy, Scotland, then Russia (in two seasons with Lada Togliatti of the elite Russian league). Riendeau was followed to Russia in the fall of 1999 by former Montreal Canadiens netminder Andre "Red Light" Racicot.

First European-trained captain of an NHL team
Lars-Erik Sjoberg, Winnipeg, 1979–80
Before Winnipeg joined the NHL it was the WHA's most powerful franchise. Far more than just the speed and slap shot of Bobby Hull, the Jets tapped the talents of Europe, becoming the first team to turn the game international with Swedes Ulf Nilsson, Anders Hedberg and Sjoberg. When Winnipeg joined the NHL in 1979–80, Sjoberb captained the Jets.

First player to captain a team for more than 15 years
Steve Yzerman, Detroit, 1986–87 to 2002–03
When Yzerman donned the Detroit "C," the NHL was still a 21-league team with clubs named the Jets, Nordiques and North Stars. Seventeen years later and it's still Yzerman's team.

First teenager to captain an NHL team
Brian Bellows, Minnesota, 1983–84
Bellows was just 19 when he was handed the leadership role on

the North Stars, after an injury to captain Craig Hartsburg early in 1983–84.

First 16-year-old to play in the NHL

Bep Guidolin, Boston, November 12, 1942

During World War II, NHL teams replenished their short rosters by picking up recruits regardless of age. Without the 18-year age restriction on players, Guidolin was too young to go to war but not to play NHL hockey. He was one month shy of his 17th birthday when called up by Boston.

First grandson of an NHLer to play in the NHL

Craig Patrick, California, 1971–72

If hockey has any bluebloods, it's the Patricks. Craig is the son of Lynn Patrick, who was the son of Lester Patrick—one of the game's founding fathers. Craig's brother Glenn was the NHL's second grandson in 1973–74, with St. Louis.

First player to have a moustache

Andy Blair, Toronto, 1930s

It was only a small one beneath Blair's nose, but it still qualifies as an NHL first for the Toronto forward. Defenseman Garth Boesch of the Leafs was the next player to join the moustache club. He sported a slim, Mandrake the Magician-style moustache during the early 1940s.

First players to have beards

Muzz Patrick, Art Coulter, NY Rangers, 1938–39

The first NHLer to sport a full beard was "Cowboy" Bill Flett in the 1970s, but 30 years before Flett's bushy display, Patrick and Coulter grew more modest stubble to win a wager with Rangers coach Lester Patrick.

First player to wear glasses

Russ Blinco, Montreal Maroons, 1930s

It's appropriate that a guy named Blinco would be the first NHLer to hit the ice with specs. The slick centre was the NHL rookie of the year in 1934 and won a Stanley Cup in 1935.

First player to popularize the slap shot
Bernie "Boom Boom" Geoffrion, Montreal, early 1950s

Geoffrion was probably not the first player to use a slap shot, but he was the first to make the shot famous. In turn, the shot gave him his famous nickname. In his biography, *Boom Boom,* the Montreal legend says he developed his slapper in junior hockey. One day, a sportswriter named Charlie Boire watched Geoffrion as he took big windups and fired away at the net in an empty arena. When Geoffrion missed the net, there would be the crack of the puck hitting his stickblade, then another crack when the rubber bounced off the backboards. To Boire, the twin cracks sounded like "boom" and "boom." "I'm going to nickname you Boom Boom," said Boire. Over 16 NHL seasons, Boom Boom and his big blaster did the rest.

First player to break one of Bobby Orr's 14 NHL records

Tom Bladon, Philadelphia, December 11, 1977

Just four years after Orr scored seven points to set the single-game points record by a defenseman, Bladon caught lightning and counted four goals and four assists in an 11–1 win against Cleveland. As Bladon confessed: "It's almost embarrassing to say you took away one of Orr's records. He was so much better than the rest of us, it was ridiculous."

First player to break one of Wayne Gretzky's 61 NHL records

Ray Bourque, NHL All-Star game, February 6, 2000

At the time of Gretzky's retirement, the Great One had his name
on 61 NHL records, including the mark of 12 All-Star game assists,
which he shared with four others. The record was broken first by
Bourque, when he assisted on a goal by Tony Amonte at 12:14 of
the second period. Bourque was followed five minutes later by
Mark Messier, who notched his 13th assist on a Ray Whitney goal.

**First player to break one of Wayne Gretzky's 61 NHL records in
regular-season play**

Adam Oates, Washington, Philadelphia, 2001–02

Gretzky's career record of 15 overtime assists was broken by playmaker Adam Oates, who racked up three overtime helpers with
the Capitals and Flyers in 2001–02 to jump ahead of Gretzky.

First NHL player to die as a result of an on-ice injury

Bill Masterton, Minnesota, 1968

The North Stars centre died in hospital, two days after fractur-
ing his skull in a game against California on January 13, 1968.
Masterton's demise resulted in more players wearing helmets
for protection.

Last player to play every position in one game

King Clancy, Ottawa Senators, March 31, 1923

In Game 2 of the 1923 Stanley Cup finals between Ottawa and
Edmonton, Clancy was recruited to replace hurting defensemen
George Boucher and Eddie Gerard, winded centre Frank Nighbor,
injured left-winger Cy Denneny and exhausted right-winger
Punch Broadbent. The sophomore was then called upon to take
the net when Clint Benedict drew a penalty. In those days, goalies
were forced to serve their own penalty time. As Benedict passed

Clancy on his way to the box and handed him his goalie stick, he uttered the now famous line: "Here kid, take care of this place till I get back."

Last player to play a full season and not draw a single penalty
Craig Ramsay, Buffalo, 1973–74
During his 14-year career, Ramsay recorded only 210 penalty minutes, a squeaky-clean average of just 15 minutes per season. He twice notched penalty-free years, in 1971–72's rookie campaign of 57 games, and in 1973–74, when he played all 78 games and recorded 46 points.

First player to play on four NHL teams, one season
Dennis O'Brien, Minnesota, Colorado, Cleveland, Boston, 1977–78
This is a stumper. After seven seasons and change with Minnesota, O'Brien was released by the North Stars, claimed on waivers by Colorado, then traded to Cleveland and, finally, claimed on waivers by Boston. O'Brien dressed for 22 per cent of NHL clubs in 1977–78.

First player to play on five defunct NHL teams
Chuck Arnason, 1971–72 to 1978–79
Arnason carried around some heavy karma during his NHL career. Five of the eight NHL clubs he dressed for failed: the Atlanta Flames, Kansas City Scouts, Colorado Rockies, Cleveland Barons and Minnesota North Stars.

Only player to play for all NHL franchises, career
Vic Lynn, 1942–43 to 1953–54
No modern-day player could (or would want to) duplicate Lynn's travel itinerary. He played for all six teams of the Original Six.

First player to play with 10 different teams
Michel Petit, 1982–83 to 1997–98
During a 16-year career, Petit was traded five times, signed as a free agent on three occasions and claimed on waivers once. He moved between teams in midseason a record five times. A strong, speedy skater with good skills, Petit's downfall was his lack of focus, which explains why he played so long—827 games—but with so many teams: Vancouver, the New York Rangers, Quebec, Toronto, Calgary, Los Angeles, Tampa Bay, Edmonton, Philadelphia and Phoenix.

First player to play 20 NHL seasons
Dit Clapper, Boston, 1927–28 to 1946–47
Clapper survived 20 seasons, first as a forward, then on defense and finally as a player-coach during his last two seasons. He played just six games in 1946–47, his 20th year, before retiring February 12, 1947.

First player to play 25 NHL seasons
Gordie Howe, Detroit, Hartford, 1946–47 to 1979–80
Mr. Hockey is the only NHLer to play one quarter-century or more. Howe played 25 years in Detroit and one season, his 26th, in Hartford, in 1979–80.

First player to receive one million votes in All-Star balloting
Jaromir Jagr, Pittsburgh, January 2000
The Czech superstar received 1,020,736 votes, by far the highest total since fan balloting began in 1985–86. The previous high of 620,788 votes was set by Detroit's Paul Coffey in 1995.

Only player to wait 17 years before receiving his first All-Star selection

Steve Yzerman, Detroit, 2000

Despite six consecutive 100-point seasons during the late 1980s and early 1990s, Yzerman didn't get his first All-Star selection until age 35. The Red Wings veteran earned First All-Star team status with a 79-point season in 1999–2000, his 17th NHL season.

First player inducted into the Hall of Fame without the mandatory three-year waiting period

Dit Clapper, 1947

Of the 10 Hall of Famers who hold this distinction (including Howe, Orr, Gretzky and Lemieux), Clapper is the least famous, and unfairly so. A rare talent, he starred for the Boston Bruins at right wing during his first 10 years in the league and then on defense for the last 10 years of his career, earning First All-Star team honours at both positions. Clapper retired February 12, 1947, and was inducted immediately into the Hall.

First player to come out of retirement after being inducted into the Hall of Fame

Gordie Howe, 1946–47 to 1979–80

Detroit's desk job for Howe after his retirement in 1971 wasn't exactly what the Hall of Famer had in mind. So Howe quit, and, just a year after his induction into the Hall in 1972, came back at age 45 to play with his sons Mark and Marty for the WHA Houston Aeros.

CHAPTER 6

Smoking
guns

In a 1988 New Year's Eve game,

Mario Lemieux gunned down the

New Jersey Devils to become the first NHLer to

score goals in five different ways. Lemieux

connected at even-strength, on the power play,

shorthanded, on a penalty shot and into the empty

net in an 8–6 Penguins win.

First NHL goal scorers

Joe Malone, Montreal, December 19, 1917
Dave Ritchie, Montreal Wanderers, December 19, 1917
Without conclusive proof of start times in the first NHL games, Malone and Ritchie share this honour. Malone scored at 6:30 of the first period in a 7–4 win against Ottawa. Ritchie scored at 1:00 of the first period in a 10–9 win against Toronto.

Last NHL goal scorer of the 20th century
Brett Hull, Dallas, December 31, 1999

Hull scored the last goal of the millennium at 8:49 of the third period, about 9:30 p.m. Central Time in Dallas. In one of only two games scheduled that night, Hull got his in typical, dramatic fashion, notching the tying and winning goals in a 5–4 victory over Anaheim—his 600th and 601st career markers. It was his 900th NHL game. "I wanted 600 in 900 games because they're round numbers and it's easier to do the math," joked Hull.

First NHL goal scorer of the 21st century

Sergei Krivokrasov, Nashville, January 1, 2000
Based on start times of the seven NHL games on tap, the first goal of the new millennium was scored by Krivokrasov at 0:22 of the first period in a 3–2 victory over San Jose.

First player to score an empty-net goal

Cecil Dillon, NY Rangers, January 12, 1932
Boston coach Art Ross replaced goalie Tiny Thompson with an extra attacker with the Bruins trailing the Rangers 4–3 late in the 10-minute overtime period. The strategy failed. Ranger winger Cecil Dillon put the puck in the empty net to cap a 5–3 victory and earn himself a place in history.

First player to score a penalty-shot goal
Ralph Bowman, St. Louis Eagles, November 13, 1934
Bowman was awarded the NHL's first penalty shot and the
Eagles defenseman capitalized, beating Montreal Maroons
goalie Alex Connell. Since it was the first goal of his career,
Bowman also became the first player in history to score his first
goal on a penalty shot.

Last player to score his first NHL goal on a penalty shot
Reggie Savage, Washington, November 18, 1992
Three players besides Ralph Bowman have registered their first
goals on penalty shots, including Phil Hoene (December 11, 1973),
Ilkka Sinisalo (October 11, 1981) and Savage. His penalty-shot
marker was one of only five goals in his 34-game career. It came
in a 5–4 Capitals win against Minnesota.

Only player to score his final NHL goal on a penalty shot
King Clancy, Toronto, November 14, 1936
In his Hall of Fame career, Clancy scored 136 times, his last goal
coming on his only penalty shot during his last game. Chicago's Mike
Karakas was Clancy's victim in the 6–2 Toronto win.

First player to score an overtime goal
Joe Malone, Montreal, January 5, 1917
Malone's historic goal came off a rebound on a Didier Pitre shot
to the side of the net that Ottawa goalie Clint Benedict failed to
clear. By accounts of the day, Malone beat Benedict "with a slow
shot" after 17 minutes of overtime in the 6–5 win.

First player to score an overtime goal after introduction of four-on-four play in 1999–2000

Mike Ricci, San Jose, October 7, 1999

Ricci scored the NHL's first overtime winner in four-on-four play against Edmonton, in a 3–2 win. Ricci's goal was on the power play, a four-on-three situation. The first true four-on-four (with neither team being penalized) was scored by Calgary's Valeri Bure on October 13, 1999.

First player to score an overtime penalty-shot goal

David Legwand, Nashville, December 23, 2000

The NHL had regular-season overtime from November 1917 until December 1942, when it dropped the concept. The league renewed the practice in 1983, but it wasn't until 2000 that a goal was scored on a penalty shot in OT. Legwand was awarded his freebie after he was dragged down from behind by New York Rangers defenseman Tomas Kloucek with 1:43 left in overtime. Legwand beat goalie Kirk McLean with a shot to the short side. Nashville won 3–2.

First defenseman to lead his team in goals, one season

Carol Vadnais, Oakland Seals, 1969–70

Vadnais was one of the few offensive threats on the lowly Seals. He led all players with 24 goals—three more than forward Earl Ingarfield. Vadnais's 44-point total was second-highest among NHL defensemen in 1969–70, a mere 76 points behind Boston's Bobby Orr. Only one other blueliner has since duplicated the feat: Kevin Hatcher of the Washington Capitals scored 34 times to tie forward Kelly Miller in 1982–83.

First player to score a hat trick in his first NHL game

Alex Smart, Montreal, January 14, 1943

The 24-year-old winger got his big-league shot in 1942–43. In his first game, Smart scored three times in a 5–1 win over Chicago. In the dressing room after the match, reporters noted his casual way, "but you could see he was inwardly glowing. The weary years of waiting (in the amateur ranks) were behind him." Unfortunately, the press was a little blinded by that glow. Despite this remarkable debut, Smart didn't stick with Montreal. His NHL career lasted only eight games.

Last player to score a hat trick in his first NHL game

Real Cloutier, Quebec, October 10, 1979

It might have been Cloutier's first NHL game, but he was no rookie. A five-year veteran and two-time scoring champion with the WHA Quebec Nordiques, Cloutier proved that the rival league had quality players. He scored 42 goals in his first NHL season, including this celebrated hat trick in a 5–3 loss to Atlanta.

Only player since 1966–67 to score a hat trick before his 19th birthday

Jaromir Jagr, Pittsburgh, February 2, 1991

Few teenagers have displayed such an explosive mixture of skills as Jagr. The Czech phenom was 13 days short of his 19th birthday when he posted three goals in a 6–2 Penguins win over Boston.

Only defenseman to score four hat tricks, one season

Bobby Orr, Boston, 1974–75

Did Orr have the Midas touch, or what? In 1974–75, the Boston golden boy rang up a quartet of three-goal games, an unheard of total by a defenseman. Orr's outbursts came in a 5–5 tie against Pittsburgh, a 6–0 romp over California and 10–4 and

8–2 demolitions of Washington. At the time, the single-season record for hat tricks was seven, held by Phil Esposito and Joe Malone.

First teenager to score five goals, one game
Don Murdoch, NY Rangers, October 12, 1976
In only his fourth NHL game, Murdoch became the toast of Broadway after bombing Minnesota goalie Gary Smith for five goals. He was just two weeks shy of his 20th birthday.

First player to record a five-goal game, with all of his team's goals
Sergei Fedorov, Detroit, December 26, 1996
Fedorov owns this first after notching all of Detroit's goals in a 5–4 win against Washington's Jim Carey.

Only defenseman to score five goals, one game
Ian Turnbull, Toronto, February 2, 1977
Turnbull remains the only rearguard to post a five-goal game. He did it in a 9–1 massacre of Detroit. His record-setting fifth goal came late in the third period on a planned play, after he took a breakaway pass from his Leafs defense partner, Borje Salming.

First player to score 10 overtime goals, career
Steve Thomas, 1984–85 to 2002–03
This NHL first had Mario Lemieux written all over it. But Thomas took advantage of Lemieux's three-year retirement while No. 66 was stuck at nine career OT goals. In 1999– 2000, Thomas scored three more to raise his career total to 11 and leapfrog past Lemieux.

Only player to score 10 points, one game

Darryl Sittler, Toronto, February 7, 1976

Sittler's mark stands alone. The Maple Leafs captain busted loose for six goals and four assists against Boston rookie goalie Dave Reece in an 11–4 scorefest.

First player to record a plus-10, one game
Tom Bladon, Philadelphia, December 11, 1977

"Everything was in slow motion," is how Bladon described his record-setting plus-10 night. His explosion of four goals and four assists broke defenseman scoring records and led the Flyers to an 11–1 mauling of the Cleveland Barons. "That's probably the way Gretzky saw the ice all the time. I got to see it like that for one night," Bladon told the *Globe and Mail*.

First 20-goal player with six different teams, career
Ray Sheppard, Buffalo, NY Rangers, Detroit, San Jose, Florida, Carolina, 1987–88 to 1999–2000

Sheppard played honest every night and on every team he was traded to during his 13-year career. Never flashy, he was the quintessential workhorse, ringing up 25 goals on his sixth team, Carolina, in 1998–99.

First player to score 20 goals in the minor leagues and the NHL, one season
Joe Mullen, St. Louis, 1981–82

Mullen spent 27 games with the Salt Lake Golden Eagles before finally joining the Blues for good in 1981–82. He scored 21 goals with the CHL club and 25 in his 49 games with St. Louis, a hockey first.

First player to score 30 goals with five different teams, career

Mike Gartner, Washington, Minnesota, NY Rangers, Toronto,
Phoenix, 1979–80 to 1997–98

Gartner became the first five-team 30-goal man in 1996–97 after notching 32 goals with Phoenix.

First rookie to score 30 goals, one season

Nels Stewart, Montreal Maroons, 1925–26

One of the league's longest-standing offensive records, Stewart's 34-goal rookie standard lasted 45 years. Gilbert Perreault finally broke Stewart's mark with 38 goals in 1970–71. Perreault needed 78 games, more than double Stewart's count of 36 games.

First player to score 40 goals with three different teams

Frank Mahovlich, Toronto, Detroit, Montreal, 1956–57 to 1973–74

There are a few big-name guns with lots of air miles who hit 40 goals with three teams, including Pierre Larouche, Joe Mullen and Dino Ciccarelli. But Mahovlich preceded this exclusive group by 12 years, scoring 40 goals once each with Toronto, Detroit and Montreal. The Big M got his third 40-goal season in 1971–72.

First modern-era player to record a goals-to-assists differential greater than 40, one season

Brett Hull, St. Louis, 1990–91

Hull delivered a monster differential of 41 on 86 goals and 45 assists in 1990–91, besting Joe Malone's 40 (44 goals and four assists) in 1917–18, when assist totals were rarely counted with any accuracy.

First player to score 50 goals on a non-playoff team

Bobby Hull, Chicago, 1968–69

Even though the Golden Jet netted a career-best 58 goals and

107 points in 1968–69, the Blackhawks finished last in the East Division and missed the postseason for the first time in a decade.

First player to score 60 goals on a non-playoff team
Denis Maruk, Washington, 1981–82
No small feat considering the team he played for. The Capitals were 15 games under .500. Maruk's 60 goals ranked third in the NHL, behind only Wayne Gretzky and Mike Bossy. His 136-point total was the fourth highest.

First player to score 70 goals on a non-playoff team
Mario Lemieux, Pittsburgh, 1987–88
Lemieux and Maruk are the only players to score more than 60 goals for teams that failed to make the playoffs. Lemieux hit 70 on the button in 1987–88, and also won the scoring title with 168 points. Despite all that gaudy offense, the Penguins went golfing in April.

Last players to score 70 goals, one season
Alexander Mogilny, Buffalo, 1992–93
Teemu Selanne, Winnipeg, 1992–93
Selanne and Mogilny each scored 76, the last time anyone cracked the 70-goal plateau.

First player to score 100 goals, one season, including playoffs
Wayne Gretzky, Edmonton, 1983–84
If you include the postseason, a few players have cracked the 90-goal barrier, including Jari Kurri (90), Brett Hull (97) and Mario Lemieux (97), but only Gretzky has hit 100—scoring 87 regular-season goals and 13 playoff markers in 1983–84.

First defenseman to record 100 assists, one season

Bobby Orr, Boston, 1970–71

Leetch. Bourque. Potvin. Coffey. Among the greatest offensive rearguards, only Orr shattered 100, amassing a career-high 102 assists in 1970–71.

First 100-point players on a non-playoff team

Bobby Hull, Chicago, 1968–69
Gordie Howe, Detroit, 1969–69

In a span of 10 days in March 1969, Hull and Howe became the second and third players (after Phil Esposito) in history to record 100-point seasons. Shortly after, when their teams failed to make the playoffs, this first became a reality. Hull scored 107 points and Howe 103. It was Howe's only 100-point campaign.

First player to score 250 power-play goals

Dave Andreychuk, Tampa Bay, November 15, 2002

Andreychuk broke Phil Esposito's NHL record of 249 career power-play goals with a first-period marker against the San Jose Sharks. Esposito was in attendance for the historic moment, covering the game on the Lightning radio network. Said Espo: "A power-play guy has to pay the price. He has to stand there and take a beating. Dave takes a beating. That's why he has 250. He's the man."

First player to break 250 points, one season (including playoffs)

Wayne Gretzky, Edmonton, 1984–85

Combining his 208 points in the regular season and 47 in the playoffs gives the Great One an unimaginable 255 points. He never broke 250 again, "struggling" between 224 and 240 combined points during his best years.

First player to finish in the top-10 scorers for 20 consecutive seasons
Gordie Howe, Detroit, 1949–50 to 1968–69
Howe didn't become the NHL's all-time scoring king with fat 70-goal seasons. In fact, Mr. Hockey never even registered a 50-goal year. No, Howe amassed 801 career goals with 20-, 30- and 40-goal seasons, never once falling below the top 10 in a two-decade span from 1949–50 to 1968–69. More remarkable, Howe finished among the top-five scoring leaders in every one of those 20 seasons.

First father-and-son tandem to finish among top-10 scorers
Syl Apps Sr. and Syl Apps Jr.
Bobby and Brett Hull are the more famous father-son duo in this category, but first came the Apps. Syl Sr. recorded multiple top-10 finishes between 1936–37 and 1947–48 with Toronto. Syl Jr. repeated his father's scoring endeavours in 1973–74 and 1975–76 with Pittsburgh.

First scoring line to finish one-two-three in scoring race
The Kraut Line, Boston, 1939–40
Nicknamed the Kraut Line because all three players had German backgrounds, Boston's trio of Milt Schmidt (52 points), Woody Dumart (43) and Bobby Bauer (43) became the first line to sweep the first three spots in the scoring race.

First scoring line with three 100-point men, one season
The Triple Crown Line, Los Angeles, 1980–81
In 1979–80, Kings coach Bob Berry teamed Marcel Dionne, Dave Taylor and Charlie Simmer as his first line. The following season the trio exploded: Dionne collected 135 points, Taylor, 122 and Simmer, 105.

First scoring line to record 200 points, one season

The Pony Line, Chicago, 1943–44

Although the Pony Line moniker originally applied to Chicago's
Max Bentley, Doug Bentley and Bill Mosienko, it was after centre
Max Bentley was traded to Toronto early in 1943 and replaced by
Clint Smith that the line did its most damage. Smith, Bentley
and Mosienko recorded 219 points in 1943–44, breaking the
old mark of 183 set by the Boston Bruins' Dynamite Line of Dit
Clapper, Cooney Weiland and Dutch Gainor in 1929–30. The
Chicago unit's record didn't last long, though. Montreal's Punch
Line—Elmer Lach, Toe Blake and Maurice Richard—broke it the
next season, with 220 points.

First scoring line to record 300 points, one season

The Nitro Line, Boston, 1970–71

Phil Esposito, Ken Hodge and Wayne Cashman became the
most explosive offensive force in NHL history in 1970–71. Pow-
ered by Espo's record-setting 152 points, the hulking threesome
tallied 336 points. The feat was even more amazing considering
Hodge and Cashman rarely played on the Bruins' power play.

Only player to score 1,000 goals, 2,000 assists and 3,000 points, career, including playoffs

Wayne Gretzky, 1979–80 to 1998–99

The chances of a second player duplicating Gretzky's fire-power
are slim to nil. In NHL action, the Great One collected 1,016 goals,
2,223 assists and 3,239 points.

CHAPTER 7

Cooler
kings

At one time, the big scorers fought

their own battles. Gordie Howe, Ted

Lindsay, Rocket Richard and Bobby Orr all topped

100 penalty minutes in a season several times. The

first wave of stone-handed thugs rolled in during

the 1970s, and penalty-minute stats exploded. Can

you say Dave Schultz?

First player penalized 100 minutes in 10 seasons

Ted Lindsay, 1944–45 to 1964–65

Lindsay was a rare package of skill and ferocity. He rang up more than 100 PIM in nine of 10 years between 1949–50 and 1958–59, then added a 10th with Chicago in 1964–65 *after* four years in retirement. "Terrible" Ted registered 173 minutes in his last season, only four shy of Carl Brewer's league-high total. His record of 10 seasons with 100 penalty minutes lasted 20 years, when it was eclipsed by Tiger Williams.

First player penalized 100 minutes in 19 consecutive seasons

Dale Hunter, 1980–81 to 1998–99

Hunter was an ornery cuss, with awesome staying power. He topped the century mark in penalty minutes every year of his career: a record 19 straight.

First player penalized 1,000 minutes
Red Horner, 1928–29 to 1939–40

The six-foot, 190-pound hardrock defenseman became the first NHLer to rack up 1,000 career minutes after leading the loop in penalties a record eight straight seasons (from 1932–33 to 1939–40). He reached the milestone in 1936–37, two years before Eddie Shore.

First player penalized 1,000 minutes with one team

Red Horner, Toronto, 1928–29 to 1939–40

Horner's record of 1,254 penalty minutes with the blue-and-white lasted 20 years, until it was snapped by an unlikely contender: Montreal's Maurice Richard, who ended his career in 1959–60 with 1,285 PIM.

First player penalized 2,000 minutes

Bryan Watson, 1963–64 to 1978–79

Ted Lindsay held the NHL record with 1,808 penalty minutes until Bugsy passed him. Watson broke the 2,000-PIM barrier in 1976–77, his 14th NHL season. He barely beat Dave Schultz to the milestone. The Hammer became the second NHLer to top 2,000 PIM in 1977–78, in just his seventh season.

First player penalized 2,000 minutes with one team

Terry O'Reilly, Boston, 1971–72 to 1984–85

Boston retired O'Reilly's No. 24 in 2001–02. No Bruin ever battled harder. O'Reilly reached the 2,000 mark in 1984–85, his last season. He retired with 2,095 penalty minutes, every one of them served in a Boston uniform.

First player to compile 2,500 penalty minutes and 500 goals

Pat Verbeek, Detroit, 2001–02

Verbeek wasn't nicknamed the Little Ball of Hate for nothing. Only five foot nine, he was always good in heavy traffic. Verbeek joined the 500-goal club in 1999–2000, with the Red Wings, and hit the 2,500-PIM plateau in 1993–94, with Hartford.

First player penalized 3,000 minutes

Tiger Williams, 1974–75 to 1987–88

Tiger cracked 3,000 minutes early in 1984–85, with Detroit. He retired with an NHL record 3,966 PIM (34 minutes shy of 4,000)—the equivalent of 66 full games.

First player penalized 3,000 minutes with one team

Rob Ray, Buffalo, 1989–90 to 2002–03

On January 3, 2002, at Calgary's Saddledome, Ray rang in the New Year with a gasket-popping, third-period outburst in which he picked up a minor, major, misconduct and game misconduct. Amazingly, not a single Calgary player was penalized during Ray's rampage. The 27 minutes pushed him over the 3,000 mark.

First player to set the single-season penalty-minutes record with three teams

Dave "Tiger" Williams, Toronto, Vancouver, Los Angeles
Williams was hell on wheels everywhere he touched down. He set the Leafs' record with 338 PIM in 1976–77, the Canucks' mark with 343 PIM in 1980–81 and, in his 13th NHL season, the Kings' standard with 358 PIM. None of these team records have survived, but the legend of the Tiger lives on.

First player penalized 100 penalty minutes, one season

Joe Hall, Montreal, 1917–18
The Montreal bad man hit the 100-minute mark right on the nose, the same spot Hall hit a lot of opposing players. Amassing 100 penalty minutes may not sound like much, but the schedule in 1917–18 was only 22 games.

First player to compile 100 penalty minutes and 50 goals, one season

Vic Hadfield, NY Rangers, 1971–72
Only five players had 50-goal years before Hadfield became hockey's reigning bad-boy sniper. He recorded 50 goals while collecting 142 minutes.

First player to compile 100 penalty minutes and 100 points, one season

Bobby Orr, Boston, 1969–70
Orr may have been a class act, but he didn't shy away from the

rough stuff. He led the Big Bad Bruins in penalty minutes with 125 in 1969–70, while topping the NHL with 120 points.

First rookie to lead the league in penalties
Mike McMahon, Montreal, 1943–44

McMahon was called up from the minors during the 1943 playoffs to add muscle to the Montreal lineup. At a solid five foot eight, 215 pounds, he had some to spare. The next season, McMahon was a regular on the Canadiens blueline, playing 42 games, recording 24 points and logging a league-high 98 penalty minutes.

First goalie to earn his team's first-ever fighting major
Billy Smith, NY Islanders, October 21, 1972

Battlin' Billy was known for his combative style; anyone who stood in his crease risked getting chopped across the ankles. As Smith once said: "I just try to give myself a little extra working room." He wasn't averse to dropping the gloves, either. On this occasion, Smith duked it out with New York Rangers winger Rod Gilbert.

First player penalized 200 penalty minutes, one season
Lou Fontinato, NY Rangers, 1955–56

Leapin' Louie became the first Ranger to top the penalty parade in 1955–56, amassing an NHL-record 202 penalty minutes. The defenseman led the league in box time on three occasions during his nine-year career.

First player to compile 200 penalty minutes and finish among the top-10 scorers
Terry O'Reilly, Boston, 1977–78

This is a difficult feat. Only three players have done it in more than 80 years: O'Reilly in 1977–78, Kevin Stevens in 1991–92 and Brendan Shanahan in 1993–94. O'Reilly logged 211 PIM and 90 points, seventh best in the league, one point behind Mike Bossy.

First players to compile 200 penalty minutes and 50 goals, one season

Kevin Stevens, Pittsburgh, 1991–92
Gary Roberts, Calgary, 1991–92

Stevens and Roberts unwittingly battled all season for this NHL first. Stevens collected 54 goals and 254 penalty minutes, while Roberts had a 53–207 count.

Last player to compile 200 penalty minutes and 50 goals, one season

Keith Tkachuk, Phoenix, 1996–97

Since 50-goal scorers Gary Roberts and Kevin Stevens hit heavyweight box-time totals in 1991–92, a few other snipers have toyed with the 200-minute mark, including Brendan Shanahan in 1993–94 and Tkachuk, who bagged 52 goals and 228 minutes in 1996–97.

First player to compile 200 penalty minutes and 100 points, one season

Kevin Stevens, Pittsburgh, 1991–92

Who else? Stevens had the best scoring punch in the game. Playing part sniper and part tough guy as Mario Lemieux's wing man, his performance in 1991–92 still looms large. He racked up this NHL first with 123 points and 254 minutes.

First player penalized 300 penalty minutes, one season

Dave Schultz, Philadelphia, 1973–74

Until Schultz, the average goon was piling up 200 minutes per season. Schultz's version of soft hands was bare knuckles. In 1973–74, he fought his way to a record 348 PIM.

First rookie penalized 300 minutes, one season
Denis Polonich, Detroit, 1975–76

Polonich was one of the smallest agitators the NHL has seen, a hot-blooded needler. At five foot six, 166 pounds, he prided himself on his willingness to throw them with anyone. In 1975–76, he became the first rookie to top 300 penalty minutes with 303 PIM. Two years later, Polonich's aggravating habits caused Wilf Paiement to slash him in the face. The incident provoked a lawsuit that earned Polonich a then-unheard-of settlement of U.S.$850,000.

Only player to compile 300 penalty minutes and 40 goals, one season
Al Secord, Chicago, 1981–82

After being traded to Chicago, Secord developed into an elite power forward. Skating on a line with Denis Savard and Steve Larmer in 1981–82, he scored 44 times while logging 303 minutes in the box.

First player penalized 400 penalty minutes, one season
Dave Schultz, Philadelphia, 1974–75

Schultz's fans at the Philadelphia Spectrum wore Nazi helmets, which was fitting—he was the closest thing to a war criminal the NHL has produced. The Hammer pounded out 472 ugly minutes in 1974–75, a record that looks as far out of reach as Wayne Gretzky's 92-goal season.

First penalty leader to lead by a margin of 100 minutes, one season

Howie Young, Detroit, 1962–63

Motor City fans dubbed Young the "Wild Thing." The name fit; Young was a kamikaze. He obliterated Lou Fontinato's single-season record for penalty minutes in 1962–63, belting it from 202 to 273. He also led runner-up Carl Brewer by 105 minutes, the second-largest margin of all time behind Dave Schultz's 196-minute bulge in 1974–75.

Last penalty leader to lead by a margin of 100 minutes, one season

Peter Worrell, Florida, 2001–02

Where have all the goons gone? In 2001–2002, Worrell had no competition for the PIM crown. The big Panthers winger spent 354 minutes behind bars to become just the third player to lead the NHL by 100 minutes—the first to do it since Dave Schultz in the mid-1970s. In second spot with 254 minutes was Worrell's teammate Brad Ference.

Only penalty leader to score 35 goals, one season
Tiger Williams, Vancouver, 1980–81

As goons go, Williams was among the best. He could give you the shivers *and* score. He led the Canucks with 35 goals in 1980–81, while amassing a league-high 343 penalty minutes. The 30-goal mark has never been breached by another NHL penalty leader.

Only player penalized 10 times, one game

Chris Nilan, Boston, March 31, 1991

"Knuckles" Nilan was born in Boston and, as any Bruins fan

knows, was born to play there. Alas, he spent most of his career with the hated Habs. In 1990–91, after a three-year stint with the equally hated Rangers, Nilan was finally traded to the Bruins. In the last game of that season he left Beantowners something to remember him by: the NHL's first and only 10-penalty game. Nilan ran roughshod over the Hartford Whalers, picking up six minors, two majors, one misconduct and one game misconduct.

First player penalized more than 40 minutes, one game
Jim Dorey, Toronto, October 16, 1968
In just his second NHL game and his first appearance at Maple Leaf Gardens, the angelic-looking Toronto rookie went after the Pittsburgh Penguins like an attack dog, collecting four minors, two majors and two misconducts before he was finally tossed with a game misconduct. The 48 PIM and nine penalties in a game were new NHL records. Dorey's NHL black marks have since been surpassed, but both are still Toronto highs.

Only player penalized more than 60 minutes, one game
Randy Holt, Los Angeles, March 11, 1979
Holt was title-holder of several records after this red-haze rampage against the Philadelphia Flyers, in which he was sentenced to 67 minutes (longer than a regulation game) on one minor, three majors, two misconducts and three game misconducts.

Only team to lead in penalty minutes in 10 consecutive seasons
Philadelphia Flyers, 1971–72 to 1981–82
The Flyers ruled the realm of rowdy for 11 straight years before relinquishing the crown to the Eddie Johnston-coached Pittsburgh Penguins in 1982–83.

First team penalized 1,000 minutes, one season

Montreal Canadiens, 1953–54

No one remembers the Habs of the 1950s as a rough bunch.
Maybe we should. In 1953–54, Montreal became the first team
to break 1,000 penalty minutes, led by none other than Maurice
Richard, who posted a team-high 112 PIM.

First team penalized 2,000 penalty minutes, one season
Philadelphia Flyers, 1980–81

It wasn't one of Fred Shero's mayhem-bent mobs from the mid-1970s
that set this milestone. Pat Quinn was at the helm when Philly pushed
the goon-o-metre to 2,621 penalty minutes in 1980–81. The second-
place Rangers were a distant 640 minutes back.

First team with four 200-penalty-minute players, one season

Philadelphia Flyers, 1972–73

The Flyers may have been playing in the City of Brotherly Love,
but there was nothing brotherly about their game plan: intimidation. The Broad Street Bullies thumped out a record 1,756
penalty minutes. The assault was led by Dave Schultz (259), Bob
Kelly (238), Andre Dupont (215) and Don Saleski (231). Only the
Blues' Steve Durbano (209) stopped a Flyers sweep of the top-
four spots on the penalty chart.

Only team with three 300-penalty-minute players, one season

Buffalo Sabres, 1991–92

The psycho Sabres racked up an all-time NHL record 2,713 PIM
in 1991–92. The major felons were Rob Ray (354), Gord Donnelly
(316) and Brad May (309).

Only team with 15 100-penalty-minute players, one season

Pittsburgh Penguins, 1988–89

What happened? Were the Pens taking nasty pills? Under abrasive rookie coach Gene Ubriaco, Pittsburgh set new NHL records with 2,670 penalty minutes and a whopping 15 players with 100 PIM. No one can say it wasn't a team effort; the only regular who didn't spend at least 100 minutes in the cooler was Phil Bourque, with 97. Even mild-mannered guys like Mario Lemieux (100), Paul Coffey (195) and Dan Quinn (102) got in on the act. Still, of 15 players, only lead goon Jay Caulfield topped 200 minutes.

First team penalized 200 minutes, one game

Minnesota North Stars, February 26, 1981

Minnesota turned the corner in 1980–81, evolving from a talented but soft team into a talented and hard team. Minnesota had its coming-out party at the Boston Garden, a rink where it hadn't won since joining the NHL 13 years earlier. The fighting broke out seven seconds after the opening face-off and escalated from there. Midway through the first period, 12 players had already been ejected for brawling. When the dust settled, the North Stars had racked up a record 211 minutes and the Bruins, 195. Although Boston won 5–1, the North Stars had proved something to themselves. Minnesota swept the Bruins in the first round of the playoffs and went all the way to the finals.

Last two teams penalized 300 minutes, one game

Calgary Flames vs Anaheim Mighty Ducks, December 8, 2001

It wasn't a '70s-style bench-clearing brawl, but it was heavy-fisted enough to crack 300 minutes—a mark not broken since Montreal and Buffalo pounded each other for 321 minutes April 12, 1992. Calgary and Anaheim's fight night at the Calgary

Saddledome resulted in six game misconducts, 19 fighting majors, 309 penalty minutes and 12 games' worth of suspensions. Calgary won the penalty count with a single-period record of 190 minutes, but lost the game 4–0. Anaheim goalie Jean-Sebastien Giguere lost credit for the shutout when he was tossed late in the game with a misconduct.

First two teams penalized 400 minutes, one game
Minnesota North Stars vs. Boston Bruins, February 26, 1981
The Bruins–North Stars tilt reaped a record 406 minutes of box time. It occurred in the first year of automatic game misconducts for anyone leaving the bench to fight. Before that, the rule was a double minor for the first man over. Everyone else could join in unpunished.

Last bench-clearing brawl
Boston Bruins vs. Quebec Nordiques, February 26, 1987
The last full-scale battle of the benches was a good old-fashioned mêlée at Boston Garden. The Bruins–Nordiques ice riot, which resulted in nine ejections and 167 penalty minutes, came after Boston city council rejected a proposed city ordinance allowing police to arrest athletes for assault during games. Boston won the slugfest 6–2.

CHAPTER 8

No
mercy

On January 23, 1944, the Detroit

Red Wings sliced and diced the

last-place New York Rangers to become the first

and only NHL team to score 15 unanswered goals

in a game. Virtually abandoned by his teammates,

Rangers goalie Ken "Tubby" McAuley was pelted

with 58 shots in the 15–0 shellacking.

First team to score 3,500 goals in a decade

Edmonton Oilers, 1980s

With Wayne Gretzky directing the assault, the high-powered Oilers amassed a record 3,526 goals in 725 games from January 1, 1980 to December 31, 1989. That works out to a sizzling average of 4.9 goals per game for the decade.

Only team to lead the league in goals in 10 consecutive seasons

Montreal Canadiens, 1953–54 to 1962–63

The Edmonton Oilers of the 1980s strung together six straight seasons as the NHL's top scoring team, but Montreal dominated the league for 10 consecutive years off the blades of Maurice Richard, Jean Béliveau, Bernie Geoffrion and Dickie Moore.

First team to score 400 goals, one season

Edmonton Oilers, 1981–82

Led by Wayne Gretzky, who compiled an NHL record 212 points, the Oilers pumped in 417 goals, surpassing the previous high of 399 set by Boston in 1970–71. The Oilers would top 400 goals in five straight seasons in the 1980s. No other team has breached the 400-goal barrier.

First team to allow 400 goals-against, one season

Washington Capitals, 1974–75

Talk about capital punishment. Washington set all kinds of records in its inaugural season; and none that it was proud of. The Caps allowed a whopping 446 goals in the 80-game schedule. The record for futility still stands.

First team to score 100 more goals than any other team, one season

Boston Bruins, 1970–71

The most explosive Bruins team of the era was the 1970–71

edition. They scored 399 times during the regular season, an astounding 108 more goals than runner-up Montreal, the eventual Cup-winner.

First team to score 200 more goals than it allowed, one season
Montreal Canadiens, 1976–77
Boston came close to the 200-goal mark with a goal differential of 192 on 399 goals-for and 207 goals-against in 1970–71. But Montreal, in 1976–77, with Ken Dryden tending the net and the big three of Larry Robinson, Serge Savard and Guy Lapointe on defense, allowed just 171 goals, while up front Guy Lafleur, Steve Shutt and company scored 387 times, a differential of 216 goals.

Last team to lead the NHL in goals scored and goals allowed, one season
Chicago Blackhawks, 1947–48
Two-way play just wasn't in Chicago's game book as it fired a league-high 195 goals and gave up a league-worst 225 goals-against. Doug Bentley finished third in scoring with 57 points, and goalie Emile Francis suffered through a tough season in the nets with a 3.39 GAA.

Only team to average less than a goal per game, one season
Chicago Blackhawks, 1928–29
The Blackhawks needed a seeing-eye dog to find the net. They scored only 33 goals in 44 games and were shut out 20 times, including a record eight games in a row. Believe it or not, winger Vic Ripley was the only Hawk to pot more than six goals. He had 11.

First team with more than 10 20-goal scorers, one season
Boston Bruins, 1977–78
Don Cherry's lunch-bucket brigade spread the scoring around. Boston broke the previous record of 10 20-goal scorers shared by the 1970–71 Bruins and the 1974–75 Canadiens. Bob Miller became the record-setting 11th Bruin to join the 20-goal club when he scored into an empty Toronto net in the second-last game of the season.

Last team with 10 20-goal scorers, one season
St. Louis Blues, 1980–81
No St. Louis team has ever scored like the 1980–81 Blues. The club's 10 20-goal scorers accounted for 300 of the Blues' franchise-high 352 goals.

First team with three 20-goal defensemen, one season
Washington Capitals, 1992–93
After a series of trades and injuries decimated its forward lines, Washington's blueline corps took over to become the highest-scoring defense in NHL history, tallying 95 goals, or 29 per cent of the team's total output of 325 goals. Kevin Hatcher scored 34, Al Iafrate, 25 and Sylvain Cote, 21.

First team with four rookie 20-goal scorers, one season
Minnesota North Stars, 1976–77
The North Stars iced four rookies—Glen Sharpley (25), Roland Eriksson (25), Steve Jensen (22) and Alex Pirus (20)—with promising futures. Oddly, this marked career highs for all but Jensen, who later scored 23 goals in 1978–79 with the Los Angeles Kings.

First team with five 30-goal scorers, one season

Chicago Blackhawks, 1968–69

There was a lot of finger-pointing after Chicago finished dead last in the tough East Division in 1968–69, especially considering its 280-goal output, which was second only to Boston's 303 goals. Chicago's scoring machine was sparked by Stan Mikita, Eric Nesterenko, Dennis Hull and Kenny Wharram, who each netted exactly 30 goals, while Bobby Hull established an NHL-record 58 goals.

First team with two 50-goal-scorers, one season

Boston Bruins, 1970–71

Considering that only three players in history had scored 50 goals prior to 1970–71, this double dip was quite a shock. The Bruins ran amok, amassing 399 goals—an incredible 96 more than the previous NHL record, which Boston set in 1968–69. Phil Esposito led the blitz with 76 goals, while Johnny Bucyk counted 51.

Last team with two 50-goal scorers, one season

Pittsburgh Penguins, 1995–96

The 50-goal scorer appears to be on the endangered-species list. Not since 1970–71, when Boston iced hockey's first 50-goal teammates, has the NHL gone so long without a pair of 50-goal men. Pittsburgh's Mario Lemieux scored 69 goals and Jaromir Jagr potted 62 in 1995–96.

First team with three 50-goal scorers, one season

Edmonton Oilers, 1983–84

This was offense from a different dimension. Wayne Gretzky tallied 87 goals, Glen Anderson, 54 and Jari Kurri, 52. This same trio of Oilers would repeat the feat in 1985–86.

Last team with four 100-point scorers, one season

Pittsburgh Penguins, 1992–93

Only a few clubs can boast four 100-or-more-point teammates in a season. Boston did it first in 1970–71, Edmonton managed it three times during the 1980s and Pittsburgh accomplished it most recently with Mario Lemieux (160 points), Kevin Stevens (111), Rich Tocchet (109) and Ron Francis (100).

First team to win 500 games in a decade
Montreal Canadiens, 1970s

The Canadiens won 501 games from January 1, 1970 to December 31, 1979, an all-time high for a decade. Montreal's record in 790 games was 501–159–130, a sparkling .716 winning percentage. The next-closest team is the Boston Bruins, who posted 487 wins in the 1970s.

First team to win 60 games, one season

Montreal Canadiens, 1976–77

Scotty Bowman's most important strategy might have been keeping his ridiculously talented Montreal team motivated though 80 games. The Canadiens lost only eight times all season.

First teams to lose 70 games, one season

San Jose Sharks, 1992–93

Ottawa Senators, 1992–93

Ottawa fans may shake their heads reading this, remembering their team's 70 torturous losses of 1992–93. Take heart, centurions. The Senators didn't lose their 70th until April 13, five days *after* the Sharks lost their 70th of the season April 8. San Jose and Ottawa are the last teams to score 25 points or less during one season; each recorded 24 points in 1992–93.

Only team to win 10 consecutive games from the start of the season

Toronto Maple Leafs, October 7 to October 28, 1993

Toronto picked up where it left off after 1993's impressive play-offs, rattling off a record 10 straight wins with Doug Gilmour, Dave Andreychuk and Wendel Clark providing the fire-power and Felix Potvin barring the door in nets. Toronto's performance broke the eight-game mark set by the 1934–35 Maple Leafs and equalled by Buffalo in 1975–76.

Only team to lose 10 consecutive games from start of the season

New York Rangers, October 30 to November 27, 1943

Decimated by World War II call-ups, the Rangers stumbled out of the starting gate with 11 straight defeats. They finally broke the string in an improbable fashion, holding mighty Montreal to a 2–2 draw November 28. The first-place Habs were riding a 12-game undefeated streak at the time. The Rangers didn't get their first win until December 12, when they downed Boston 6–4. New York won only six games all season.

Only team to be unbeaten in the first 15 games of the season

Edmonton Oilers, 1984–85

The defending champions came out of the gate firing on all cylinders. Edmonton's undefeated streak of 15 straight games (12–0–3) broke a 41-year record set by Montreal (11–0–3) in 1943–44, and propelled the Oilers to a first-place finish in the West with a 49–20–11 record.

First team to win more than 15 consecutive games, one season

Pittsburgh Penguins, March 9 to April 10, 1993

Sparked by Mario Lemieux's return after missing 24 games for cancer treatments, Pittsburgh steamrolled its opponents in a record 17 straight games during the final four weeks of 1992–93. The Penguins broke the league-high 15-game effort set by the New York Islanders in 1981–82.

First team to lose more than 15 consecutive games, one season
Washington Capitals, February 18 to March 26, 1975
It probably wasn't a champagne day, but when the Capitals ended their horrific 17-game losing streak they also snapped a 44-year-old NHL record for defeats dating back to 1930–31, when the Philadelphia Quakers lost 15 in a row.

Only team to go unbeaten in 35 consecutive games, one season
Philadelphia Flyers, October 14, 1979 to January 6, 1980
For 11 weeks, the Flyers refused to lose. Pat Quinn's club racked up 25 wins and 10 ties during the streak, breaking the previous mark of 28 games without a defeat set by the 1977–78 Canadiens. The Flyers' record-setting 29th game was a 5–2 road victory over Boston on December 22, 1979.

Only team to go winless in 30 consecutive games, one season
Winnipeg Jets, October 18 to December 20, 1980
The NHL was a reality check for Winnipeg after dominating the rival WHA. In their second NHL season, the Jets won only nine games and suffered the longest winless streak ever, losing 23 and tying seven in a nine-week ride of desperation.

First team to record a 100-point season
Detroit Red Wings, 1950–51
Led by scoring champion Gordie Howe, this Motown machine amassed 101 points (44–13–13). Although Detroit topped the 100-point mark in only the second season of the 70-game schedule, it proved a tough barrier to crack. Over the next

18 years, only two teams—the 1951–52 Red Wings and the 1955–56 Canadiens—reached the century mark, both with exactly 100 points. It wasn't until 1968–69, with an expanded 76-game schedule, that the Claude Ruel-coached Canadiens finally broke the Red Wings' record.

First team to finish 15 games above .500 during the regular season and not make the playoffs
Montreal Canadiens, 1969–70

Unlucky just doesn't cover it. The Canadiens missed the playoffs despite being 16 games *above* the .500 mark. The reason was the NHL's unbalanced playoff format between the powerful East and weak West Divisions.

First team to post a 50-point single season improvement
Quebec Nordiques, 1992–93

Breakout years from Joe Sakic and Mats Sundin keyed Quebec's jump from 52 points in 1991–92 to 104 points in 1992–93, a 52-point leap. Only San Jose has topped this mark, improving its 1992–93 record by 58 points, from 24 to 82 points.

Only team to suffer a 40-point decline, one season
Detroit Red Wings, 1970–71

In Gordie Howe's last year in Motown, the Wings plunged like clay pigeons, going from 95 points in the previous season to 45. The record-setting tumble broke Chicago's 38-point decline in 1953–54. Detroit's fall was a symptom of management rot. Its farm system was in disarray, and the hiring of college coach Ned Harkness to run the show didn't help. During Harkness's four-year reign as coach and GM, Detroit never made the playoffs.

Only team to score more than 15 goals in a game
Montreal Canadiens, March 3, 1920

The Flying Frenchmen found a goalie to their liking in Quebec rookie Frank Brophy. They embarrassed the Bulldogs backstop in a 16–3 massacre.

Only team to record 40 scoring points, one game
Buffalo Sabres, December 21, 1975

Buffalo has recorded a couple of 14-goal games in franchise history, but its 14–2 win against the woeful Washington Capitals marked the first and only time any team has been credited with 40 scoring points, on 14 goals and 26 assists. The Sabres' best period was the third, when they exploded for eight goals and 15 assists.

First team to record a point for losing a game
Edmonton Oilers, October 7, 1999

In 1999–2000, the NHL introduced a new system of rewarding one point for a tie in regulation time and two points for an overtime win. Although most fans enjoy the five-minute overtime period, the new system has changed things. For example, it is now theoretically possible for a team to fail to win a single game all season and still make the playoffs: 82 ties might do it. Edmonton was credited with one point for a regulation tie, despite losing 3–2 in overtime to San Jose.

CHAPTER 9

Pipe
dreams

Until February 7, 1976, Dave Reece had a promising NHL career. The Boston goalie owned a 7–4–2 record, with two shutouts. But all that unravelled when Toronto's Darryl Sittler lit him up for six goals and four assists on national TV in an 11–4 rout. The league had its first 10-point player and Reece had his walking papers.

First goalie to face 25,000 shots
Patrick Roy, 1984–85 to 2002–03

Roy has seen more rubber during his career than the Trans-Canada Highway. Since 1982–83 (when shot stats became available), he is the only NHL netminder to handle more than 25,000 shots, including his 25,000th on April 8—his second-last shot of 2000–01—in a 4–2 win against Minnesota. It was Roy's 16th season.

First goalie to face more than 2,000 shots, one season (since 1982–83)
Greg Millen, Hartford, 1982–83

A few goalies—including Dominik Hasek and Grant Fuhr—thrived on the workload, but the 2,000-shot season is still a lot of puck to face. In Toronto, the Maple Leafs burned out Felix Potvin with three 2,000-shot seasons in four years. During the first year shots were officially recorded, 1982–83, Millen faced 2,056 shots in 60 games for the Whalers. He averaged 34.2 shots—five more per game than the league average of 29.1.

Only goalie to face 70 shots and not lose, one game
Ron Tugnutt, Quebec, March 21, 1991

Tugnutt owns the distinction of not losing a game with the greatest shots-against (73), in a 3–3 tie with Boston.

First goalie to face 80 shots, one game
Sam LoPresti, Chicago, March 4, 1941

LoPresti handled a league-record 83 shots from Boston marksmen and stopped 80. Despite the sterling performance, his teammates failed to score more than two goals in the 3–2 Bruins win.

First goalie to make 20,000 saves (since 1982–83)

Grant Fuhr, 1981–82 to 1999–2000

Fuhr beat out Patrick Roy, John Vanbiesbrouck and Curtis
Joseph, the next three 20,000-save netminders, recording his
20,000th career stop during 1996–97 while backstopping
St. Louis. Roy and Vanbiesbrouck each hit 20 grand in 1999–
2000, Joseph in 2002–03.

First goalie to make 2,000 saves, one season

Curtis Joseph, St. Louis, 1992–93

Since shot totals became available in 1982–83, only a handful
of netminders can claim 2,000 saves. Joseph did it first, with
2,006 saves on 2,202 shots and 196 goals.

First goalie to record 400 wins

Terry Sawchuk, 1949–50 to 1969–70

After 15 seasons and 388 career wins, Sawchuk was traded to
Toronto, where he recorded the league's first 400th win by a
backstopper February 4, 1965, in a 5–2 victory against Montreal.

First goalie to record 500 wins

Patrick Roy, 1984–85 to 2002–03

The NHL's first 500th win belongs to the game's best netminder
today. Roy earned the milestone in classic style with Colorado,
blanking Dallas 2–0 for his 59th career shutout December 26, 2001.

First goalie to record 30 wins in eight consecutive seasons

Martin Brodeur, 1991–92 to 2002–03

Brodeur and Patrick Roy were vying for this first after they tied
Tony Esposito with seven straight 30-win seasons in 2001–02.
Brodeur, on his way to legendary status as one of hockey's great
netminders, won his 30th game of 2002–03 with a 3–2 win

against Minnesota on February 9, 2003. Six weeks later, Roy tied Brodeur, notching his eighth straight 30-win season with his 30th win for Colorado on March 22, 2003. It came in an 8–1 victory against Chicago.

First goalie to record four 40-win seasons
Martin Brodeur, New Jersey, 1991–92 to 2002–03
In 2002–03, the Devils netminder posted a league-high 41 wins for his fourth 40-win season. Only two other goalkeepers in league history—Terry Sawchuk and Jacques Plante—have ever won 40 games three times. Amazingly, Brodeur came within an eyelash of posting six consecutive 40-win campaigns between 1997–98 and 2002–03. In 1998–99, he won 39 games; in 2001–02, 38.

First goalie to record 40 wins, one season
Terry Sawchuk, Detroit, 1950–51
It didn't take long after the 70-game schedule was introduced in 1949–50 for a netminder to break the 40-win barrier. But Sawchuk's 44-win total is even more impressive, considering he was a rookie. No freshman goalie has broken that mark—not even in today's 82-game schedule.

Last goalie to record 45 wins, one season
Bernie Parent, Philadelphia, 1973–74
Philadelphia's championship team of goons had a few genuine stars, including Parent, who was key to coach Fred Shero's decree: "If you keep the opposition on their behinds, they don't score goals." The logic was that the Flyers could only take as many penalties as they did because Parent shut the door in most shorthanded situations. In 1973–74, Philadelphia won 50 games and Parent received credit for 47 victories, the first and last time a netminder has cracked the 45-win mark.

Last goalie to record all his team's wins, one season

Ron Low, Washington, 1974–75
Kirk McLean, Vancouver, 1994–95

McLean notched all 18 wins in the lockout-shortened 48-game season. Low is the last netminder in a full season of play to record all of his club's victories—eight wins by the Capitals in the 80-game schedule.

First goalie to record 350 losses

Gump Worsley, 1952–53 to 1973–74

Only two puck stoppers have had a long enough shelf-life to lose more than 350 games. Gilles Meloche amassed 351 losses—just one less than Worsley's record 352. The Gumper's 350th loss came in his final season, 1973–74.

First goalie to record 40 losses, one season
Harry Lumley, Chicago, 1950–51

Another product of the modern 70-game schedule was the 40-loss barrier, suffered first by Lumley during Chicago's darkest days. His 41-loss total wasn't the worst, though. The next season the Hawk netminder recorded a record 44 defeats. For Lumley, fresh from a Stanley Cup with Detroit in 1950, his two-year ordeal in Chicago must have been hell on earth.

Last goalie to record 40 losses, one season

Marc Denis, Columbus, 2002–03

The Blue Jackets can thank Denis for helping set a team record of 29 wins in 2002–03, but their workhorse netminder also joined the unsavoury ranks of 40-loss NHL goalies. Denis got shelled with a league-high 2,404 shots and made 2,172 saves during an NHL record 4,511 minutes between the pipes. Denis was put through the wringer and came out the team's MVP.

First goalie to allow 300 goals, one season
Ken McAuley, NY Rangers, 1943–44
McAuley can thank World War II for his NHL start, but the minor leaguer might have done better serving overseas than between the pipes. Playing all 50 games of the schedule, McAuley won just six times and was ventilated for an all-time-high 310 goals. By comparison, next worst is Hartford's Greg Millen, who gave up 282 goals in 60 games during 1982–83.

Only goalie to allow a goal five seconds into his first game
Paul Skidmore, St. Louis, December 20, 1981
Things went sour for Skidmore fast in his first NHL start. The Blues rookie barely had time to blink before Winnipeg's Doug Smail intercepted an errant pass and snapped home a wrist shot. It was the fastest goal from the start of a game in NHL history. A shaken Skidmore was beaten again at 1:43 by Paul MacLean, as Winnipeg went on to win 5–4. Skidmore got his first big-league win nine days later in a 6–1 victory over Hartford, but that was his last NHL appearance.

First goalie to record a shutout
Georges Vezina, Montreal, February 18, 1918
Vezina recorded the first NHL shutout in a 9–0 win against the Toronto Arenas. It was the 29th game of the league's first season, 1917–18.

First goalie to post a shutout in his first NHL game

Hal Winkler, NY Rangers, November 16, 1926

Winkler, 34 years old and a veteran of the western pro leagues, played only 75 NHL games but registered 21 shutouts, his first in his first game, a 1–0 win against the Montreal Maroons.

First goalie to record more than 100 minutes of shutout hockey from start of career

Dave Gatherum, Detroit, October 11 and 16, 1953

Unknown Gatherum owns the NHL record for the longest shutout sequence by a first-time goalie. Promoted from Sherbrooke, he replaced an injured Terry Sawchuk for three games in October 1953, registering a 4–0 shutout against Toronto in his October 11 debut. In Chicago five nights later, Gatherum held the fort until 00:21 of the third period when the Hawks scored. Gatherum earned the 2–2 tie and set the shutout mark at 100 minutes and 21 seconds from the start of a career. The next evening he won 2–1, but his career record of 2–0–1 meant little with Sawchuk due to return. Gatherum never played another NHL game.

Last goalie to shut out all opposing NHL teams at least once, one season

Ed Giacomin, NY Rangers, 1966–67

This is the kind of record that could only be set during the NHL's six-team era. No goalie today could hope to repeat Giacomin's feat of shutting out all opposition teams at least once. He recorded a league-best nine zeroes, blanking Toronto three times, Chicago and Detroit, twice and Montreal and Boston, once.

First goalie to post shutouts with six different teams, career

Lorne Chabot, 1926–27 to 1936–37

It may have been Chabot's mercurial temperament that got him traded six times in 11 seasons, but his netminding was beyond reproach. Chabot won two Stanley Cups and recorded an amazing 73 shutouts spread over six teams. Sean Burke is the only other six-team shutout goalie.

First opposing goalies to record their first career shutouts in the same game

Zac Bierk and Michael Leighton, Phoenix vs. Chicago, January 8, 2003

The NHL has seen more than 150 scoreless games since 1917–18, but never a 0–0 duel between two netminders without a previous shutout. Neither Bierk nor Leighton had netted a goose egg before this scoreless tie in January 2003. Bierk stopped 40 shots and Leighton, 31. It was also Leighton's first NHL contest.

First goalie to stop a penalty shot

George Hainsworth, Toronto, November 10, 1934

The league's first penalty shot (taken by Montreal's Armand Mondou) was stopped by Hainsworth, who made the save to preserve a 2–1 win. According to the rules, the shot had to be taken from within a 10-foot circle, 38 feet from the net.

First goalie to face two penalty shots, one game
Roy Worters, NY Americans, December 11, 1934

In the first season of the newly adopted penalty-shot rule, referees called numerous infractions, but few of the free shots resulted in goals. Worters became the first goalie to face two in a game, stopping drives by Eddie Shore and Dit Clapper. New York still lost, 4–3 to Boston.

First goalie to play 20 NHL seasons

Terry Sawchuk, 1949–50 to 1969–70

Sawchuk backstopped for 21 seasons. It's a wonder he survived, as David Dupris explains in *Sawchuk:* "Terry played in an era when goalie equipment was small, archaic, almost dangerous to use. There were no goalie coaches, agents, nutritionists, physiotherapists or physical trainers. The goalies of Terry's time learned alone, toiled alone and excelled alone, on sheer talent and determination."

First goalie to play 1,000 games

Patrick Roy, 1984–85 to 2002–03

On January 20, 2003, Roy added another milestone to his amazing resume by playing in his 1,000th NHL game. The Colorado goaltender made 29 saves and was chosen first star in the 1–1 tie against Dallas. In a ceremony before the game, Roy noted: "My objective was just to survive in the league. That's what I was hoping, and here I am 18 years later in a position to be the first one to ever hit 1,000. It's great."

First goalie to play for eight different teams

Gary Smith, 1965–66 to 1979–80

Smith earned the nickname "Suitcase" backstopping Toronto, Oakland (which later became California), Chicago, Vancouver, Washington, Minnesota and Winnipeg.

First goalie to play with three different teams, one season

Jim Rutherford, 1980–81

Rutherford played on four teams in his 457-game career, three of them after trades in 1980–81, when he stopped for coffee in Detroit for 10 games, Toronto for 18 and Los Angeles for three. He posted a 9–16–4 record in 31 games.

First goalie to play 90 games, one season (including playoffs)

Bernie Parent, Philadelphia, 1973–74

Parent led the league in almost every category for goalies in 1973–74, including wins (47), shutouts (12) and goals-against average (1.89). His Cup-winning playoff performance wasn't too shabby, either. In all, the Flyers netminder played 73 regular-season and 17 playoff games. His 90th game came May 19 in a 1–0 shutout against Boston, the first time a modern-day expansion team won the Stanley Cup.

Last goalie to play every minute of every game, one season

Ed Johnston, Boston, 1963–64

Johnston didn't miss a minute of action through the 70-game schedule of 1963–64. He led the league in minutes (4,200) and in losses (40), with Boston winning just 18 times and finishing last in the six-team NHL. Roger Crozier was the last goalie to appear in every game in a season. He played ironman through all 70 contests, except for 32 minutes of a possible 4,200 in 1964–65.

First NHL goalie to score a goal
Billy Smith, NY Islanders, November 28, 1979

Smith was credited with the NHL's first goal by a netminder after an errant pass by Colorado Rockie Rob Ramage ended up in his own net. The net had been vacated on a delayed penalty call to the Islanders. After Smith stopped the puck, Ramage picked it up and fed a blind pass back, only to have the puck slide the length of the ice and into his own net.

First goalie to shoot and score a goal

Ron Hextall, Philadelphia, December 8, 1987

The ever-mobile Hextall had long predicted he would shoot and score a goal. He even practised his coast-to-coast shot. In just his second NHL year, the moment came when Chicago, down two goals late in the game, pulled their netminder. Hextall aimed, fired it rink-length and scored his league first.

First goalie to score a power-play goal
Evgeni Nabokov, San Jose, March 10, 2002
With Vancouver goalie Peter Skudra pulled in favour of an extra attacker, Nabokov directed a pin-point shot 190 feet into an empty net, recording hockey's first power-play marker by a net-minder. The goal came on a 5-on-4 man-advantage at 19:12 of the third period in the Sharks' 7–4 win.

First goalie to score a game-winning goal
Martin Brodeur, New Jersey, February 15, 2000
Brodeur was the last Devils player to touch the puck after Philadelphia forward Daymond Langkow unintentionally directed it into his own net. Goalie Brian Boucher was on the bench during a delayed penalty. Brodeur's fluke goal proved the winner in New Jersey's 4–2 win.

First goalie to score a goal and record a shutout, one game
Damian Rhodes, Ottawa, January 2, 1999
Rhodes is the fifth NHL netminder to score a goal but the first in a shutout win. The Ottawa netminder was credited with the goal during a delayed penalty when New Jersey's Lyle Odelein misplayed the puck into his own net. Rhodes was the last Senator to touch the puck. He outscored the Devils in the 6–0 win.

First goalie to receive credit for an assist
Tiny Thompson, Boston, January 14, 1936
Netminders had assisted on goals before Thompson, but none

were ever given official recognition. The Boston keeper did receive credit for an assist during a 4–1 victory against Toronto in 1936, but it's possible he should have received two. The Bruins scored their last two goals on breakaways by Babe Siebert. According to the *Globe and Mail*'s game account: "Thompson was credited with assists by the official scorer on both goals scored by Siebert. He passed out to the defenseman—who was unguarded near the blueline—for the third goal, and also started the play that produced the fourth counter. It was believed the official scorer's action in giving a goaler two assists in one game constituted a precedent in the NHL, and even had the experts thumbing the record books to get the low down on goalers who in any way entered the scoring statistics." Mysteriously, despite this eyewitness testimony, the NHL today only credits Thompson with one assist in the game.

First goalie to score 10 points, one season
Grant Fuhr, Edmonton, 1983–84
On the high-flying Oilers, even the goalies outscored many opposing skaters during 1983–84. Fuhr racked up 14 points on Edmonton's record 446-goal count to become the only netminder to break the double-digit point barrier. Fuhr appeared in only 45 games that season.

First goalie to record three points, one game
Jeff Reese, Calgary, February 10, 1993
Reese's name lives on in hockey circles thanks to one night in February 1993 when the Flames bombed San Jose 13–1 and Reese tallied three assists, two off goals by Robert Reichel and one off Gary Roberts. "It was just one of those fluky things," Reese told the *Hockey News*. "All the bounces went our way. I happened to touch the puck three times. Only once did I fire it up. It

bounced off the boards and created a two-on-one. The other times I stopped the puck beside the net and the defensemen threw up the puck."

First goalie to record 100 penalty minutes, one season
Ron Hextall, Philadelphia, 1986–87

Hextall's bad-boy reputation was established during his rookie season, 1986–87, when he logged a netminding-record 104 penalty minutes. His status only grew during the playoffs that year, when the Flyer freshman earned an eight-game suspension for a wicked slash to the back of the legs of Edmonton's Kent Nilsson.

———————————————————————

First goalie to have his jugular vein slashed
Clint Malarchuk, Buffalo, March 22, 1989

In a crease collision with St. Louis rookie Steve Tuttle, Malarchuk's throat was sliced open by Tuttle's skateblade. The stricken goalie was rushed to hospital, where he received 300 stitches to close the six-inch gash. He was back in the Sabres' nets 11 days later.

———————————————————————

First goalie to cause a rule change
Clint Benedict, Ottawa, 1917–18

In the NHL's first season, goalkeepers were not legally allowed to leave their feet to make a save. Benedict didn't let that stop him: he was an expert at accidentally losing his balance and falling to smother the puck. Other goalies soon began copying Benedict's deceptive methods. In response, NHL president Frank Calder changed the rule January 9, 1918, allowing goalies to fall to the ice to make saves.

First butterfly-style goalie

Glenn Hall, 1952–53 to 1970–71

Hall was the first to break with the classic "stand-up" pose and position his legs wide apart. The spread-eagle style allowed Hall to cover more net with better manoeuvrability against deflections and rebounds.

Only ambidextrous goalie

Bill Durnan, Montreal, 1943–44 to 1949–50

With identical gloves on each hand, Durnan switched stick- and glove-hand depending on the attack. Archive film shows him flipping his stick smoothly and effortlessly from hand to hand as he crossed the crease, preparing for the shot. It is claimed he often switched his stick back and forth just to psyche out his shooters.

First European-trained goalie

Goran Hogosta, NY Islanders, November 1, 1977

Europeans were slowly trickling into the NHL ranks when Hogosta signed as a free agent in June 1977. He made NHL history just months later, replacing Billy Smith for nine minutes in the second period against Atlanta, a shared shutout 9–0 win.

First European-trained goalie to start a game

Hardy Astrom, NY Rangers, February 25, 1978

Just four months after Goran Hogosta played nine minutes as the first European in NHL nets, Astrom got this historic start. He played brilliantly, stopping Montreal's 28-game unbeaten streak in a 6–3 Rangers win.

First goalie to captain an NHL team

John Ross Roach, Toronto St. Pats, 1920s

Only six netminders have been appointed team captain in NHL

history, Roach being the first during his years with the St. Pats. Later, in 1932–33, after the NHL passed a rule stating that a team captain had to be on the ice at all times, Roy Worters wore the "C" for the New York Americans; so did George Hainsworth (Montreal), Alex Connell (Ottawa) and Charlie Gardiner (Chicago).

Last goalie to captain an NHL team
Bill Durnan, Montreal, 1947–48

After captain Toe Blake suffered a career-ending leg injury January 10, 1948, Durnan took over the Montreal captaincy, but only for the remainder of the season. He did such a responsible job—repeatedly leaving the crease to question the referee—that some teams complained, protesting that Durnan's actions slowed the game and gave the Canadiens unscheduled and strategic timeouts. As a result, prior to 1948–49, the NHL prohibited netminders from serving as captains.

First brother goalies
Len and Ken Broderick

The first goaltending brothers in the NHL were the Brodericks; Len played one game for Montreal, replacing Jacques Plante on October 30, 1957, and Ken, who played 27 games, started his first in 1969–70 with Minnesota.

First brothers to face each other as opposing goalies
Ken and Dave Dryden, March 20, 1971

In their first-ever meeting, Ken backstopped the Montreal Canadiens in a 5–2 win against brother Dave's Buffalo Sabres. After the game, the two Drydens skated to centre ice and, in an unusual gesture for regular-season play, shook hands. The Drydens faced each other six times in NHL play, including during two playoff games, another league first.

First goalie scored upon by his brother

Tiny Thompson, Boston, March 18, 1930
After playing against each for the first time, December 4, 1928, brothers Tiny and Paul Thompson made history in their 14th NHL meeting, when Paul scored on Tiny during a clash between the Boston Bruins and the New York Rangers. The goal came at 14:48 of the second period. Boston won 9–3.

First goalie to surrender his first NHL goal to his brother

Tony Esposito, Montreal, December 5, 1969
What could Tony Esposito salvage from this 2–2 tie against Boston, especially considering brother Phil scored both goals against him? Perhaps the satisfaction of the tie in his first start; and this obscure NHL first by brothers.

First position player to play goal

Harry Mummery, Quebec Bulldogs, February 4, 1920
Mummery was the first skater to replace an injured goalie. The big, lumbering Quebec defenseman replaced regular Frank Brophy, giving up five goals in a 5–0 loss to Ottawa. Mummery subbed three more times during his career and allowed a total of 20 goals for a pitiful 6.25 goals-against average.

Last position player to play goal

Jerry Toppazzini, Boston, October 16, 1960
Toppazzini is the last skater to tend goal in an NHL game. The Topper bravely subbed without pads for an injured Don Simmons, late in the third period of a 5–2 loss against Chicago.

CHAPTER 10

Crime
blotter

"**Bad boys,** bad boys, watcha gonna do when the cops come for you?" A disturbing number of NHL players and executives have run afoul of the law, and the trend appears to be on the rise. These are the kind of nasty firsts that no one wants attached to their name.

First player suspended for possession of cocaine

Don Murdoch, NY Rangers, 1978

Murdoch, nicknamed "Murder," played on the Mafia Line in
New York with Phil Esposito and Don Maloney. The 21-year-
old's bright future took a dark turn when he was caught with
4.8 grams of cocaine during a routine customs search in Toronto,
in the summer of 1978. Although he didn't get jail time, Murdoch
was suspended for the 1978–79 season. The Rangers winger was
reinstated after 40 games, but had trouble regaining peak form;
his career soon fizzled out.

First player arrested for possession of hashish

Ric Nattress, Montreal, 1983

The NHL's first stoner. The Canadiens rookie defenseman was
suspended for the 1983–84 season after he was convicted for
possession of marijuana and hashish. Nattress was reinstated
after 40 games.

First player suspended for admitting he used cocaine

Borje Salming, Toronto, September 4, 1986

Salming wasn't caught with cocaine, he merely admitted in a
newspaper interview he had tried it six years before at a party.
The NHL was not amused. It suspended the Swedish defenseman
for the 1986–87 season. However, the ban was largely a public-
relations ploy; Salming was reinstated after eight games. In 1990,
Grant Fuhr was suspended for making the same admission.

First player arrested for smuggling cocaine

Bob Probert, Detroit, March 4, 1989

Probert lived life as hard off-ice as on it. In 1989, the heavyweight champion was caught at the Windsor-Detroit border
with 14 grams of blow. The U.S. government tried to have him

deported. Probert served a 90-day jail sentence, and was re-instated by the league March 9, 1990.

Only player arrested for possessing crack cocaine
Kevin Stevens, NY Rangers, January 23, 2000

The Rangers winger was arrested with a prostitute and several grams of crack cocaine in an Illinois hotel room. Although Stevens later denied using the crack, he signed a police statement admitting he had bought the drugs. The prostitute arrested with Stevens called him "a crack monster." Stevens, who was married with two children and a third on the way, was immediately admitted into the NHL's substance-abuse program. It was his second stint in rehab. At season's end, he was signed as a free agent by Philadelphia.

Only player to admit to heroin use
Jere Karalahti, Los Angeles, January 2002

The tattooed-covered Finnish defenseman recalled his drug-taking days with a dreamy fondness in a January 21, 2002, *Sports Illustrated* interview, including the admission that he used to smoke heroin. What was it like? "Take the best orgasm you've ever had, multiply it by a thousand and you're still nowhere near it," said Karalahti. On August 16, 2002, Karalahti was suspended for six months for his third violation of the NHL's substance-abuse policy. He then left the NHL to return to play in Finland.

First player ordered into a drug treatment centre
Bob Probert, Chicago, September 2, 1994

Despite the fact he had been busted for smuggling cocaine five years earlier, Probert continued to battle various addictions. On July 15, 1994, he crashed his motorcycle into a car. He had traces of coke in his system and a blood-alcohol level three times the legal limit. He was suspended by Chicago without pay and ordered into a league-supervised treatment centre in California. Probert was reinstated by the NHL on April 28, 1995.

First convicted rapist to join an NHL team
Billy Tibbets, Pittsburgh, 2000–01
Before being signed by the Penguins, Tibbetts served three years in a Massachusetts prison for assault and battery with a deadly weapon: a BB gun. The conviction violated the terms of his parole. Two years before, Tibbetts had plead guilty to the rape of a 15-year-old girl. He received a suspended sentence and four years probation for that offense.

First player convicted of vehicular homicide
Craig MacTavish, Boston, 1984
While driving under the influence of post-practice alcohol, MacTavish rear-ended another car, propelling it into a parking lot where it collided with two other vehicles and flipped over. The driver, a 26-year-old woman, died from her injuries four days later. The Bruins forward was convicted of vehicular homicide and received a one-year jail sentence. After missing the 1984–85 season, MacTavish was traded to Edmonton, where he resumed his NHL career, eventually winning four Stanley Cups.

Only player arrested between periods
Frank Beaton, Birmingham Bulls, February 19, 1978
Between the first and second periods of a WHA game featuring the Cincinnati Stingers and the visiting Birmingham Bulls, police forced their way into the Bulls' dressing room with a warrant for the arrest of Frank "Seldom" Beaton. The Bulls enforcer was led away in handcuffs, charged with an assault committed in

Cincinnati two years before: he had broken the cheekbone of a gas-station attendant after the man accidentally spilled gasoline on his Corvette. Stingers coach Jacques Demers posted Beaton's $2,000 bond, stating: "We stick together when it comes to things like this."

First player to plead guilty to indecent exposure
Dino Ciccarelli, Minnesota, 1987

Ciccarelli went out to retrieve the newspaper from the front porch of his house—without any pants on. He was spotted by a neighbour, and wound up charged with indecent exposure. When the case went to court, Ciccarelli's lawyer stated: "He does admit that he frequently walks around the house in a nude or semi-nude state. The biggest problem is that the complaint suggests he's some kind of sexual pervert or deviant." Ciccarelli plead guilty to the misdemeanour and was sentenced to perform 50 hours of community service.

First player suspended for gambling
Babe Pratt, Toronto, January 29, 1946

Pratt was initially suspended for life for gambling on NHL games, but after an appeal, the league backtracked and reinstated the popular Toronto veteran just 15 days later. At the end of the 1945–46 season, Pratt was traded to Boston.

First players to receive lifetime suspensions for gambling
Don Gallinger, Boston, 1948
Billy Taylor, NY Rangers, 1948

Gallinger and Taylor's names surfaced on bookies' client lists during a police investigation into racketeering. They were suspended for life by NHL president Clarence Campbell for associating with known gamblers and betting on NHL games.

Unlike Pratt, they received no quick reprieve. Their banishment lasted until 1970.

Only player to receive a lifetime suspension for assaulting a referee
Billy Coutu, Boston, April 1927

Coutu was one of hockey's first crazies. He didn't like losing, or referees. He was booted out of the league for punching out referee Jerry Laflamme after Boston lost to Ottawa in the final game of the 1927 Cup final. The ban was lifted five years later, but by then Coutu was too old to play in the NHL.

First player charged with assault
Sprague Cleghorn, Montreal, March 1923

During the third period of a playoff tilt between Montreal and Ottawa, the villainous Cleghorn smacked Senators defenseman Lionel Hitchman over the head with his stick. Hitchman had to be carried off the ice, bleeding profusely. After the game, Ottawa police arrested Cleghorn and charged him with common assault. He was convicted and fined $50.

First coach sued for assault
Emile Francis, NY Rangers, November 1965

It wasn't a pretty spectacle. The Rangers coach became irate when a goal judge was slow to signal a game-tying goal by Detroit's Norm Ullman, November 21, 1965. Francis darted to the end of the Madison Square Garden arena to berate the goal judge, and ended up in a fist fight with some hecklers. Ranger players vaulted over the glass to join the fray, and the brawl escalated, before it was finally broken up by police. Francis was later sued for assault. He lost the case, and had to pay U.S.$80,000 in damages.

First player sentenced to jail time for an on-ice incident
Dino Ciccarelli, Minnesota North Stars, January 1988
Ciccarelli was charged with aggravated assault after he struck Toronto Maple Leafs defenseman Luke Richardson in the head three times with his stick during a game at Maple Leaf Gardens, January 6, 1988. Ciccarelli was sentenced to one day in jail with a $1,000 fine. He ended up doing two hours behind bars. Ciccarelli was not fazed by his stint in police custody. As he said later: "I thought it was the *Barney Miller* show. The first thing I saw was a big fat detective eating a jelly donut. Then I stood around signing autographs for the other poor guys in there."

First player suspended an entire calendar year for an on-ice incident
Marty McSorley, Boston, February 2000
The slash that McSorley delivered to the noggin of Vancouver's Donald Brashear with three seconds left in the game February 21, 2000, landed him in court. McSorley was convicted of assault and given 18 months probation. He was also suspended for the Bruins' last 23 games of the season and the playoffs. NHL commissioner Gary Bettman later extended the suspension to a full calendar year. Although McSorley was eligible to return to action February 21, 2001, no NHL team offered the 36-year-old free agent a contract.

First player suspended for making a racial slur
Chris Simon, Washington, November 8, 1997
Players had uttered racial epithets before the 1997–98 season, but they hadn't been suspended for them. Capitals tough guy

Chris Simon was—a three-game suspension for calling Edmonton's Mike Grier a "nigger" at the end of a hard-fought 2–1 game. Two weeks later, Simon's teammate Craig Berube was given a one-game suspension for calling Florida's Peter Worrell a "monkey."

First NHL owner sent to jail
Harold Ballard, Toronto, 1972

The miserly Maple Leafs boss was sentenced to three concurrent three-year jail sentences for tax evasion. But Ballard spent only one year behind bars. Unfortunately for the Leafs' franchise, he returned to power and proceeded to oversee the most embarrassing 20-year stretch in the club's history.

First players union president sent to jail
Alan Eagleson, 1997

Once hockey's most powerful man, Eagleson was fined $1 million and sentenced to 18 months in jail for swindling players and stealing disability-insurance money and profits from various Canada Cup hockey tournaments (money intended for the players' pension fund). While in prison, Eagleson (then 64 years old), fetched coffee and worked as a cleaner.

First chairman of the NHL Board of Governors sent to jail
Bruce McNall, 1997

McNall was elected to the powerful post of chairman of the NHL Board of Governors in 1992. It was a short reign. In March 1997, the Los Angeles Kings owner and fraud artist went to prison to serve five-and-a-half years for swindling banks and investors out of U.S.$250 million.

CHAPTER 11

The big
picture

When CBC first began televising

Hockey Night in Canada games in

colour, in 1966–67, stronger lighting was installed

at Maple Leaf Gardens and the Montreal Forum.

The players initially had trouble adjusting to the

glare. Some applied burnt cork under their eyes.

Toronto goalie Terry Sawchuk wore sunglasses

when sitting on the bench.

First radio broadcast of a hockey game

Toronto, February 18, 1923

Norm Albert, an editor at the *Toronto Star,* was recruited to provide the play-by-play for a senior-league game between teams from North Toronto and Midland, Ontario. He had a busy night. Toronto won by a lopsided 16–4.

The first time Foster Hewitt used the phrase, "He shoots, he scores!"

Toronto, February 16, 1923

The voice of Canadian hockey for five decades, Hewitt used his signature phrase on his first hockey radio broadcast, a playoff game between intermediate teams from Toronto and Kitchener at Toronto's 9,000-seat Mutual Arena. Hewitt described the action from a glass booth in the penalty-box area for station CFCA. The arrangement was less than ideal. The glass in the tiny booth kept fogging up and obscuring the skinny 20-year-old broadcaster's view.

First radio show to feature the three-star selection

The Hot Stove League, CBC Radio, *1936*

The three-star selection originated on *The Hot Stove League,* a radio program sponsored by Imperial Oil that advertised Imperial 3-Star gasoline. Old-time greats such as Syl Apps and Joe Primeau originally chose the three stars.

First coast-to-coast hockey broadcast in Canada

Detroit Red Wings vs. Toronto Maple Leafs, January 7, 1933

Radio listeners across Canada first heard Foster Hewitt welcome them with "Hello Canada and hockey fans in the United States and Newfoundland!" for the first time as the Maple

Leafs edged the Red Wings 7–6. The broadcast was carried coast to coast on 20 stations.

First hockey game filmed indoors
Montreal Canadiens vs. Toronto Maple Leafs, February 28, 1931
Lights! Cameras! Action! If the film of this wild 5–6 overtime tilt between the Leafs and the Canadiens at Toronto's Mutual Street Arena still exists, it would be worth seeing. The game featured loads of violence, two frantic rallies by the home team and crazed antics by overexcited fans, including one psycho who threw a heavy, horn-handed knife at referee Bert Corbeau. Toronto's Busher Jackson and Montreal's Marty Burke brawled on the ice and in the penalty box, and when Charlie Conacher got involved, a policeman joined the fray and ended up trading blows with the Leafs' star. Conacher, who was not ejected or even penalized for punching the cop, eventually scored the tying goal with a minute left in OT.

First hockey telecast
London, England, October 29, 1938
Surprisingly, the first live transmission of a hockey game took place in England, not North America. The British Broadcasting Corporation telecast the second and third periods of a game between the Harringay Racers and Streatham at London's Harringay Arena.

First hockey telecast in North America
New York, February 15, 1940
Twelve years before hockey appeared on the CBC, a game between the New York Rangers and Montreal Canadiens was broadcast from Madison Square Garden on an experimental station set up by NBC. The game did not have a large viewing audience, as there were fewer than 300 TV sets in the city.

First NHL team to regularly televise its games
Chicago Blackhawks, 1946–47
The CBC can't even claim credit for being the first network
to regularly broadcast NHL games. During the 1946–47
season, the Blackhawks televised home games on their local
station, WBKB.

First televised NHL game in Canada
Chicago Blackhawks vs. Montreal Canadiens, October 11, 1952
Hockey Night in Canada switched on its cameras for the first
time in 1952 at the Montreal Forum, as the Habs lost to the
Hawks 3–2. It was a French-language broadcast with René
Lecavalier handling the play-by-play.

First English-language *Hockey Night in Canada* broadcast
Boston Bruins vs. Toronto Maple Leafs, November 1, 1952
Hockey Night in Canada's first English-language broadcast aired
with Foster Hewitt at the mike, as Toronto edged Boston 2–1.
Only the last half of the game was televised; Leafs owner Conn
Smythe feared the broadcast would cut into the live gate. He
wasn't the only person to share this view. NHL president
Clarence Campbell called television, a "menace."

First *Hockey Night in Canada* broadcast to originate outside Toronto or Montreal
Los Angeles Kings vs. Vancouver Canucks, October 9, 1970
Hockey Night in Canada kicked off the 1969–70 season with a
telecast from Vancouver's Pacific Coliseum. The Canucks' NHL
debut against the Kings was carried coast to coast on a Friday
night. The play-by-play announcer was Jim Robson. Songstress
Juliette, whose variety show had aired after *Hockey Night in
Canada* for many years, sang "O Canada."

First use of the *Hockey Night in Canada* theme song

1968–69

"Danda-da-da-dan-da." The popular tune that has been called Canada's unofficial anthem was written by a woman. But when Vancouver-born composer Dolores Claman was asked to compose the *Hockey Night in Canada* theme, she had never even seen a hockey game. (In fact, she didn't see a game in person until 30 years later.) Still, she devised two compositions on piano. As Claman recalled: "They just said to make it like the theme of an adventure series. And then I thought of all the gear they wear, which is sort of gladiatorial, and I thought I'd make it very stirring and brave."

First appearance of Don Cherry on CBC's "Coach's Corner"
1980

The bombastic Cherry taped his first segment of "Coach's Corner" in 1980, with co-host Dave Hodge on *Hockey Night in Canada,* not long after being fired as coach of the Colorado Rockies. Cherry's straight-talking style hit a nerve among hockey viewers, and 23 years later the Prime Minister of Saturday Night is still holding forth.

First nationally televised NHL game on American television

Chicago Blackhawks vs. New York Rangers, January 5, 1957

The Americans put hockey on the tube in 1957, when CBS began showing games on Saturday afternoons. The first telecast featured the Blackhawks versus the Rangers from Madison Square Garden. CBS introduced several novel concepts, including between-period interviews with on-ice players and a showdown between NHL shooters and minor-league goalie Julian Klymkiv (whose NHL career consisted of a 19-minute stint with the Rangers in 1958.) Most important, CBS broadcast the entire game, a move not adopted by the CBC until 1968.

First pay-per-view hockey broadcast
Chicago Blackhawks vs. Minnesota North Stars, April 8, 1991
Launched during the 1991 playoffs in Minnesota, the pay-per-view concept generated huge revenues, due primarily to the North Stars' Cinderella run to the Cup finals. Viewers were charged U.S.$9.95 per game in the first two rounds and U.S.$12.95 per game for the Conference and Cup finals. The North Stars' 11 home games attracted 300,000 viewers and brought in U.S.$3.5 million.

First live HDTV telecast of a hockey game
New York Rangers vs. Buffalo Sabres, October 27, 1998
For American sports fans who have long complained they can't follow the puck on TV, high-definition television—with its wider screen and startling 3D-quality graphics—may be the answer. According to reviewers, HD hockey "showed promise and the puck" when New York's Cablevision and Madison Square Garden Network generated the first HDTV telecast at a Wiz outlet in New York. Unfortunately, the players didn't cooperate: no goals were netted in the scoreless tie, though Paul Kruse and Darren Langdon went toe-to-toe in the first high-definition fight.

First interactive NHL webcast
Pittsburgh Penguins vs. Chicago Blackhawks, January 6, 2002
Cyberhockey arrived early in 2002. This Pittsburgh–Chicago tilt was not televised, but fans with a computer and high-speed Internet access could listen to the game and watch video high-

lights on the Penguins' website, then take part in the broadcast itself by joining live chat sessions between periods.

First appearance of the FoxTrax puck

NHL All-Star game, January 20, 1996

Among the dumber ploys introduced to sell hockey to American TV viewers was the Fox network's "FoxTrax," which debuted at the 1996 All-Star game. Wherever the puck moved on-ice, it was tailed by a vibrating blue dot; when a shot was fired, the puck sprouted a red comet trail. Serious hockey fans were offended by the cartoonish graphics, and the gimmick—despite Fox's stubborn efforts—never caught on. FoxTrax was abandoned before the 1998–99 season.

First hockey player to wear a helmet cam

Kelly Hrudey, Los Angeles, September 27, 1991

Hrudey's goalie helmet was wired with a micro-camera during an exhibition game against the New York Rangers, staged on an outdoor rink in the parking lot of Caesar's Palace, Las Vegas. The innovation permitted viewers to experience hockey from a goaltender's perspective for the first time.

First hockey player followed by a TV camera for an entire game

Mario Lemieux, Pittsburgh, January 9, 2001

It was billed as "60 minutes with 66." During this Penguins–Bruins clash at Boston's Fleet Center, a camera focussed on Lemieux for the entire game, even when he was sitting on the bench. The Mario channel came complete with a stats pack detailing Lemieux's ice time, shifts, shots on goal, goals, assists, hits and hits taken, which played simultaneously on a split screen. The CTV broadcast was available only to viewers with a digital TV system. Lemieux posted his team's two goals in a 5–2 loss.

First hockey player to appear on the cover of *Sports Illustrated*
Jean Béliveau, Montreal, January 23, 1956

Sports Illustrated had been in business for two years before a hockey player graced its cover. The honour did not go to either one of the NHL's biggest stars, Maurice Richard and Gordie Howe, but to the 24-year-old Béliveau, who won his first scoring title with Montreal in 1955–56. Although it's hard to believe, the season marked the only time in his career that Béliveau won the Art Ross Trophy.

First hockey player to be named *Sports Illustrated*'s Sportsman of the Year

Bobby Orr, Boston, January 1970

Hockey rarely received much coverage in *Sports Illustrated*, but the magazine found it impossible to ignore Orr's magical 1969–70 season. No. 4 led the NHL in scoring; captured the Hart Trophy as league MVP, the Norris Trophy as outstanding defenseman, the Conn Smythe Trophy as playoff MVP, and led the Bruins to their first Cup in 30 years. To date, Orr and Wayne Gretzky (in 1982) remain the only hockey players to receive the *SI* tribute.

Only hockey player named *Sporting News'* Man of the Year

Wayne Gretzky, Edmonton, January 1982

Although the Oilers didn't win the Cup in 1982, Gretzky's eye-popping 92-goal, 212-point season convinced the *Sporting News* that he deserved its Man of the Year award.

First hockey player fined for writing a sports column

Maurice Richard, Montreal, 1953

During the 1953–54 season, Richard penned an opinionated

hockey column titled *Tour de Chapeau* (*Hat Trick*) in the Montreal French-language weekly *Samedi-Dimanche*. But Richard's comments got him in trouble when he criticized NHL president Clarence Campbell's decision to ban Bernie Geoffrion for the eight remaining games between Montreal and New York, after the Boomer broke the jaw of Ranger Ron Murphy in a stick-swinging duel. Richard called the suspension a "farce" and Campbell a "dictator." Campbell demanded and got a retraction from the Rocket, then fined the Canadiens star $1,000. The column was terminated.

First hockey player asked to pose nude for *Playboy*
Manon Rheaume, 1992
Rheaume's short stint in the nets for the Tampa Bay Lightning during a 1992 NHL preseason game earned her plenty of media attention, including a guest spot on the *David Letterman Show*. The media buzz culminated in *Playboy* offering the dark-haired French-Canadian beauty U.S.$75,000 to pose *au naturel*. Rheaume turned the magazine down, declaring: "If *Playboy* offered me a million dollars, I would still refuse."

First hockey player to appear on the cover of *Time* magazine
Lorne Chabot, Chicago, February 11, 1935
As a weekly newsmagazine since 1923, *Time* has devoted a surprising number of cover stories to athletes, though only a few of them have been about hockey players. Bobby Hull (1968), Phil Esposito (1972) and Wayne Gretzky (1985) have all graced *Time*'s familiar red-framed cover, but the first two NHLers to receive front-page treatment were a pair of old-time goalies: Davey Kerr of the New York Rangers in 1938 and Lorne Chabot of the Chicago Blackhawks, whose photo appeared on *Time*'s 1935 cover, along with the tag line "His savings are on ice." Chabot was considered

a newsworthy figure because he had replaced recently deceased
Chuck Gardiner in the net of the defending champion Blackhawks.

First hockey player to appear on a soup can
Wayne Gretzky, Los Angeles, 1996
Gretzky attained the rank of true "souperstar" in 1996, when he
became the first hockey player to appear on a Campbell's soup
can. The image of the Great One, clad in a generic hockey uniform, appeared on 50 million labels for 20 different varieties of
Campbell's chunky soup.

First hockey personality to appear on a Miller Lite beer commercial
Bernie Geoffrion, 1976
Shortly after Geoffrion resigned as coach of the Atlanta Flames,
he was asked to go to New York to shoot a beer commercial.
Geoffrion's comic timing and rubbery face made him a natural
for Miller's popular "Tastes Great! Less Filling!" campaign. In his
autobiography, *Boom Boom,* Geoffrion says he earned $20,000 for
shooting the first 30-second spot. That was serious cash. In his
16-year NHL career, the most Geoffrion earned in a season was
$27,000. Boomer's deal with Miller lasted a lucrative 13 years.

First hockey cards
C55 set, 1910–11
This 36-card issue, produced by Imperial Tobacco in 1910–11, was the
first set of catalogued hockey cards. Inserted in packs of cigarettes,
the cards featured colour images of such players as Cyclone Taylor,
Lester Patrick and Georges Vezina on the front with a pair of crossed
hockey sticks and a brief bio on the back. The C-55 cards are hard to
find today. A mint set is worth about U.S.$20,000.

First table-top hockey game

1932

The prototype was built by Don Munro in his Toronto basement. Munro was out of work during the Depression and his kids were driving him crazy, so he took some scrap metal, whittled a few wooden figures and devised the first table-top hockey game. The concept, which was first sold at Eaton's in Toronto, in 1932, was an immediate success. Munro's wooden model was produced until the mid-1950s, when it was eclipsed by a version made by Montreal's Eagle Toy Company, featuring painted tin players and metal rods that allowed the players to twirl 360 degrees.

First hockey story to be required reading for Canadian school children

The Hockey Sweater, *Roch Carrier, 1984*

Carrier's short story tells the tale of a young Quebecker whose mother orders a hockey sweater from the Eaton's catalogue in Toronto. When the sweater arrives, the boy is crushed to discover it's not the jersey of the Montreal Canadiens and his hero, Maurice Richard, but the one worn by the hated Maple Leafs. Worse, his mother insists that he wear the despised blue-and-white, much to his embarrassment and the ridicule of his chums at the local rink.

First children's song unofficially banned by the NHL

"Three Blind Mice"

It wouldn't work today with four on-ice officials, but in the 1950s this children's ditty was a favourite among arena organists, who could stir a crowd by piping out "Three Blind Mice" whenever the three officials had, in the organist's opinion, made a bad call against the home team. The nursery rhyme was banned from all rinks during the 1960s.

First goalie to record a Christmas song

Johnny Bower, Toronto, December 1965

The Maple Leafs netminder recorded a novelty children's record called "Honky the Christmas Goose" with Little John and the Rinky Dinks for the 1965 Yuletide season. The tune was written by songwriter Chip Young, and the proceeds went to charity.

First hockey player to have a top-40 song written about him

Eddie Shack, Toronto, 1966

Few players were more popular than Eddie the Entertainer in his Maple Leafs heyday. The tune "Clear the Track, Here Comes Shack" by Doug Rankin and the Secrets shot to number one on the Toronto pop charts in February 1966, ahead of tunes by the Beatles, the Rolling Stones, Elvis and all the rest. The song's lyrics were written by TV broadcaster Brian McFarlane; the music was supplied by McFarlane's brother-in-law, Bill Macauley.

First rock star to have a pro hockey team named in his honour

Jim Morrison, 1996

Larry Lane, owner of Jacksonville's 1996–97 entry in the ECHL, called his team the Lizard Kings in a tribute to Jim Morrison, the charismatic singer-lyricist of the Doors. Morrison was fascinated by dreams, death and insanity, and used these themes in his lyrics, especially in his poem "Celebration of the Lizard" ("I am the Lizard King, I can do anything").

First rock star to write a hit song about death and hockey

Tom Cochrane, "Big League," 1988

Hockey has been mythologized with both positive and negative themes, but perhaps none better than the dark twist captured in the "Big League"—the story of a young hockey star's premature death. The inspiration for the song came from a man whose son was a big Cochrane fan and a promising hockey player with an athletic scholarship. Unfortunately, the youth's dream of playing in the big leagues died with him in a car accident. Grief-stricken, the father felt he had to meet his son's musical hero. Cochrane was so moved by his fellow westerner's tragedy that he penned a song about it.

First TV sitcom to feature a regular cast member whose character was an NHL goalie

Cheers, *1987*

When the producers of NBC's *Cheers* needed a love interest for Carla Tortelli, the surly barmaid at Sam Malone's Boston watering hole, they found their Romeo in Eddie LeBec, a fictitious netminder for the Bruins. LeBec, who joined a travelling ice show as a skating penguin after his hockey career tanked, is eventually killed while saving a fellow penguin from a Zamboni gone berserk.

First TV sitcom to feature a crazed "face-painting" hockey fan

Seinfeld, 1995

During the 1995 NHL playoffs, NBC coincidentally aired a *Seinfeld* episode in which Elaine dates a hockey fan—one who paints his face red and green for New Jersey Devils games. The "face-painter" also wears a Devils sweater with the No. 30, and the name Brodeur on the back. The show was broadcast the night prior to Brodeur recording his third shutout against Boston in the Eastern Conference quarterfinals. It marked only the fifth time a goalie posted three zeroes in a best-of-seven format since 1939.

First movie to inspire the name of a scoring line
The French Connection, *1971*
Rick Martin, Gilbert Perreault and Rene Robert, all French
Canadian and all dangerous, were dubbed The French
Connection after the hit movie by Buffalo reporter Lee Coppola.

First hockey movie
The King of Hockey, *1936*
This low-budget Warners Brothers production follows the career
of Gabby Dugan as he advances from the American college
ranks to the pros. The hockey scenes were shot on a rink at the
Warner lot on Sunset Boulevard, using university players from
UCLA and USC. Unfortunately the scriptwriter was clearly un-
familiar with hockey: there were references to "fouls," "the
penalty cage" and "being down by two points."

First hockey movie to become a cult classic
Slapshot, *1977*
Regarded today as the best hockey movie ever made, *Slapshot*
received a lot of criticism for excessive violence and profanity
when it was released. The film stars Paul Newman as Reg
Dunlop, playing-coach of the Charlestown Chiefs. Newman's
character was based on real-life coach John Brophy, the Chiefs
on the real-life Johnstown Jets of the Eastern Hockey League.

CHAPTER 12

The old barn

Toronto's Maple Leaf Gardens was the first arena with elevators, goal lights, plexiglass and a painted ice surface. The Gardens also hosted a few historic lasts, including the Original Six era's last game, played May 2, 1967. The Leafs defeated Montreal 3–1 that night to capture their last Cup to date.

First arena to host a hockey game

Victoria Skating Rink, Montreal, March 3, 1875

Although Halifax also claims this historic honour, over-whelming evidence suggests Montreal hosted the first "public exhibition" of organized hockey, using, for the first time, a block of wood instead of a lacrosse ball, goals and a player to protect the goal (a goalie), a no-forward-passing rule borrowed from rugby, and a 200- by 85-foot ice surface. According to the *Montreal Gazette* in March 1875, nine players per team "wheeled and dodged each other" in an "interesting and well-contested affair."

First arena built exclusively for hockey

Westmount Arena, Montreal, 1898

Erected at the corner of St. Catherine Street and Wood Avenue by the Montreal Arena Corporation in 1914, Westmount (also known as Montreal) Arena boasted 5,000 seats, several thousand standing-room places and artificial ice. The rink served as the home for a number of celebrated Montreal hockey teams, including the Stanley Cup-winning AAA, the Shamrocks, the Wanderers and the Canadiens.

First arena built exclusively for women's hockey

Ridder Arena, Minneapolis, 2002

The construction of U.S.$20-million Ridder Arena signalled the growing importance of women's hockey. The 3,400-seat rink hosted its first women's collegiate game October 19, 2002, with the University of Minnesota Golden Gophers defeating the St. Cloud State Huskies 8–0 before 3,239 fans.

First hockey arenas in Canada with artificial ice

Denman Street Arena, Vancouver, B.C., 1911

Willows Arena, Victoria, B.C., 1911

Knowing that no pro league could survive in British Columbia's mild Lower Mainland climate on natural ice, Lester and Frank Patrick built Canada's first artificial ice rinks for their new league, the Pacific Coast Hockey Association. Far from the hockey centres in the frigid east, the PCHA began play in 1911 with three teams and two artificial ice rinks. Vancouver's Denman Street Arena was the largest in the world, with a seating capacity of 10,500.

Only arena to host its last NHL game 25 years after it was replaced

Boston Arena, February 26, 1952

When Boston Garden's ice-making plant was damaged after a section of the roof over the adjoining train station collapsed, a game between the Bruins and the Red Wings was moved to Boston Arena. The old rink had last hosted a Bruins game in 1927. Detroit won 4–3 before a modest crowd of 4,049 fans. Gordie Howe notched the game-winner, making him the answer to a tough trivia question: Name the last NHL player to score a goal at Boston Arena.

First arena associated with the phrase "hanging from the rafters"

Olympia Stadium, Detroit

The famous sports phrase is said to have originated in Detroit's famously steep-sided Olympia, where fans in the standing room-only section would literally hang from the rafters to get a better view of the game. The "Big Red Barn on Grand River" closed its doors for good at the end of the 1977–78 campaign, a season in which the Olympia established a new NHL attendance record.

First arena with a pipe organ
Chicago Stadium, 1931

The sound of a massive Barton pipe organ thundering through wooden baffles set in the ceiling of Chicago Stadium was synonymous with Blackhawks hockey for more than 50 years. The largest pipe organ in North America, it featured six keyboards, 883 stop keys and more than 40,000 pipes, ranging in size from a few inches to 32 feet. The organ's bright red-and-yellow console alone weighed seven tonnes. The sound the organ could generate was equivalent to a 2,500-piece band. However, the organ was never cranked to full volume because the roar would have smashed all the glass in the building.

First arena with a suspended time clock
Maple Leaf Gardens, Toronto, 1931

The green, four-sided Art Deco clock was one of Maple Leaf Gardens' most distinctive features. Known as the "Player's Please" clock due to its prominent cigarette ad, it hung high above centre ice, where it simply, but elegantly, indicated the time remaining, the period and the score. The clock was replaced in 1967 with something much bigger and uglier, a symbol of the end of the Original Six era.

First arena with luxury boxes
Capital Center, Washington, 1974

The arena in Landover, Maryland, boasted 40 luxury suites clustered along the stadium's upper levels. The innovation was 20 years ahead of its time. Today, every NHL team's financial health depends upon leasing these elite play-pens for obscene amounts of money.

First arena with a retractable dome

Civic Arena, Pittsburgh, 1961

Built in 1961, primarily for theatrical events, the Civic Arena became home to the Pittsburgh Penguins as of 1966–67. The stadium features the world's largest retractable dome—a 170,000-square-foot expanse. Although it would be a novel idea, the Penguins have never played a game here with the roof open.

First arena to install separate penalty boxes

Maple Leaf Gardens, Toronto, November 8, 1963

Amazingly, for 45 years, NHL players shared the same penalty box with only a middle-aged attendant to keep them apart. The Gardens' decision to create separate penalty boxes came one week after a vicious and prolonged fight broke out in the box between Bob Pulford and Terry Harper during a Leafs–Canadiens game on *Hockey Night in Canada,* October 30, 1963. Although both the Gardens and the Montreal Forum installed separate boxes in 1963–64, the league didn't make the concept mandatory until two years later.

First arena to award one of its penalty boxes to an opposition player

Boston Garden, 1994–95

During the Bruins' final season at decaying Boston Garden in 1994–95, the club began making plans to auction off and distribute arena souvenirs. Team president Harry Sinden decreed that the Garden's home penalty box would go to venerable Bruins tough guy Terry O'Reilly. Sinden also stated that the visitor's penalty box would be given to Montreal Canadiens brawler John Ferguson, who paid his first visit to the Boston sin bin 12 seconds into his first NHL game. Ferguson never did receive his gift. Someone stole it before delivery.

First arena to use a Zamboni

The Montreal Forum, March 10, 1955

This classic symbol of the Great White North was actually invented in the mid-1940s by Frank Zamboni, a rink attendant at Hollywood's Paramount Studios. Zamboni's idea for a motorized ice cleaner caught the attention of figure skater Sonja Henie, and, with her support, he was able to build a prototype. Before the Zamboni, NHL rinks were cleaned and flooded between periods by workers using shovels and barrels of water. The Zamboni made its NHL debut March 10, 1955, during a 0–0 tie between the Canadiens and the Maple Leafs at the Montreal Forum. It was a bumpy baptism. During the game, Habs fans grew so angry with the Leafs' stifling, defensive play that they littered the ice with rubbish, including pigs feet.

First arena to feature on-ice advertising

Maple Leaf Gardens, Toronto, March 1, 1978

Just days after he bought the CFL Hamilton Tiger-Cats franchise, Maple Leafs owner Harold Ballard had the Ti-Cats' snarling logo painted on the Gardens' ice surface. The move violated the NHL's rule against on-ice advertising and Ballard had to remove it, but not before he had achieved his purpose: to generate publicity for himself and his football team, and infuriate thousands of Toronto Argonaut fans.

First arena to feature rink-board advertising

Madison Square Garden, February 8, 1979

Rink-board advertising had long been a staple in Europe, but didn't appear in an NHL arena until the three-game 1979 Challenge Cup between the NHL All-Stars and the Soviet Union national team at Madison Square Garden.

Last undersized NHL arena

War Memorial Auditorium, Buffalo, 1995–96

The opening of Buffalo's Marine Midland Center in 1996–97 spelled the end for the last of the NHL's undersized rinks. War Memorial Auditorium measured 193 by 84 feet—compared to the NHL standard of 200 by 85 feet adopted in 1930. Other smaller venues included Boston Garden (191 by 83 feet) and Chicago Stadium (185 by 85 feet), both of which were replaced by the mid-1990s.

First arena named after a corporate sponsor

Los Angeles Forum, 1987

Predictably, the trend started in California. The Kings' home rink became known as the Great Western Forum in 1987 after the Great Western Bank purchased the arena's naming rights. Other NHL teams soon followed the Kings' example and dumped dignity in exchange for cash.

First arena with a microbrewery
First Union Center, Philadelphia, 1996

Hockey and beer have always been a natural combination, so it's not so surprising that an NHL team finally installed a suds factory. The Philadephia Flyers rink (formerly known as the Core States Center) not only features its own brewery (the Red Bell Brewery and Pub), it's also home to the NHL's first cigar club.

First arena to host a funeral for a hockey player

The Montreal Forum, March 11, 1937

The term "hockey shrine" took on added meaning March 11, 1937, when the Forum hosted the public funeral of Montreal Canadiens great Howie Morenz, who had died three days earlier from a coronary embolism. The funeral involved 15,000 mourners inside the Forum; another 50,000 jammed the streets outside. The last game at the Forum was played March 11, 1996, 59 years to the day after Morenz's funeral.

First arena to host an NBA game
Maple Leaf Gardens, Toronto, November 1, 1946
Surprisingly, the NBA's first game was played in Canada. The New York Knicks defeated the Toronto Huskies 68–66 in front of 7,090 fans. The Huskies lasted only one season in the 11-team NBA, finishing last in the Eastern Division.

Only arena to host an NFL game
Chicago Stadium, December 18, 1932
When a raging snowstorm struck Illinois in December 1932, NFL officials decided to move the championship game between the Chicago Bears and Portsmouth Spartans indoors. The game was played at Chicago Stadium, home of the Blackhawks. The arena's floor was covered in soil and crude line markings were painted over the surface. The Bears won the historic gridiron encounter—attended by 11,000 fans—by 9–0.

First arena to host the NHL Entry Draft
The Montreal Forum, 1980
When the draft was first opened to the public in 1980, it drew 2,500 curious spectators. It also drew some boos from Montreal fans, who watched in disbelief as their team broke with tradition and chose Regina's Doug Wickenheiser with the first overall pick, instead of Montreal Junior Canadiens French sensation Denis Savard. Wickenheiser finished with 276 career points; Savard recorded 1,338.

CHAPTER 13

Bench
wizards

Hired to be fired. It could be the slogan of NHL coaches. None of today's bench bosses have a hope of lasting anywhere near the record 20 consecutive seasons that Jack Adams piloted the Detroit Red Wings for. Maybe the men in suits get too much credit when their teams win, but they are always the first to be blamed when things go wrong.

Only coach to be fired, then re-hired two days later

Roger Neilson, Toronto, March 1979

Neilson was canned by Leafs owner Harold Ballard on a
Thursday, then secretly re-hired before a Saturday night game
with Philadelphia when the Toronto tyrant changed his mind.
But no announcement was made to the media, which left the
identity of the new Leafs coach in question right up to game time.
To milk maximum publicity out of the event, Ballard wanted
Neilson to walk out wearing a paper bag over his head, then
remove it just before the opening face-off. Neilson wisely refused.
When he appeared behind the bench at the start of the game, the
Toronto fans gave him a loud ovation. But the reprieve was short-
lived. Ballard fired Neilson again a couple of weeks later.

First coach fired after starting the season with a perfect record

Bill Gadsby, Detroit, 1969–70

Gadsby was fired by GM Sid Abel after the club defeated Toronto
and Chicago in its first two games of the 1969–70 season. Claiming he "didn't like the direction" the first-place club was headed
in, Abel took over behind the bench and promptly snapped the
streak by losing to Minnesota. But maybe Abel knew what he
was doing: Detroit logged a 17-point increase over Gadsby's total
the previous year.

First coach of two NHL teams, one season

Fred Glover, California and Los Angeles, 1971–72

The practice of hiring a recently fired coach is a product
of expansion. The last-place Golden Seals gave Glover the
boot three games into the 1971–72 season. He soon found
employment down the coast in L.A., where he replaced Larry
Regan at the 10-game mark. Glover then guided the Kings to a
last-place finish.

First black pro hockey coach

John Paris Jr., 1970s, 1980s, 1990s

As well as being pro hockey's first black coach, during his more than 24 years behind the bench Paris was named top coach in five different hockey leagues, including the IHL and CHL.

First NHL coach to change lines on the fly
Odie Cleghorn, Pittsburgh Pirates, 1925–26

Cleghorn introduced the tactic of changing lines on the fly as playing-coach of the expansion Pittsburgh Pirates in 1925–26. Cleghorn realized that his young team lacked experience, but was blessed with a number of fast skaters. To enhance this advantage, Cleghorn not only began changing lines on the fly, but was also the first NHL coach to regularly alternate two forward lines. Until this time, teams had generally played with one unit most of the game. The strategy helped Pittsburgh to a surprising third-place finish.

First coach to pull his goalkeeper for an extra attacker

Art Ross, Boston, March 26, 1931

Ross pulled goalie Tiny Thompson—for an extra attacker—in the last minute of play in Game 2 of the Cup finals against the Montreal Canadiens. The "amazing manoeuvre" as the papers dubbed it, did not pay off. Montreal beat the Bruins 1–0.

First coach to pull his goalkeeper for an extra attacker during a delayed penalty

Milt Schmidt, Boston, October 20, 1960

Schmidt is believed to have introduced what would become standard hockey strategy. He pulled netminder Don Simmons

and added forward Bronco Horvath in mid-play, after referee
John Ashley signalled a delayed penalty against Detroit.

First coach to pull his goalie with his team leading
Tommy Ivan, Detroit, March 21, 1954
Detroit was pounding Toronto 6–1 late in the third period of the
final game of the 1953–54 season when Ivan pulled goalie Terry
Sawchuk and sent out an extra attacker. Weird? Sure it was, but
the Red Wings coach was trying to help Sawchuk win the Vezina
Trophy for fewest goals-allowed and the $1,000 prize money that
went with the award. At that point, Sawchuk had allowed one
more goal than Leafs netminder Harry Lumley, so if the Wings
scored again the pair would be tied. But Lumley held off Detroit
and won the trophy. The next season, Sawchuk turned the tables
on Lumley, slipping past the Leafs goalie on the last night of the
schedule and claiming the award by a margin of two goals.

First coach to take a turn as goalie
Odie Cleghorn, Pittsburgh Pirates, February 23, 1926
The best known story of a coach stepping into the breach during
a game is Lester Patrick and his 46 minutes of playoff glory for
the Rangers in 1928. But before Patrick came Cleghorn, who
replaced goalie Roy Worters for one game late in the 1925–26
season. The Pirates edged Montreal 3–2 with Cleghorn between
the pipes, then won six of their next seven games to squeak into
the playoffs. Ironically, the man who replaced Patrick as the
Rangers' coach when Patrick entered the net in 1928 was—wait
for it—Cleghorn.

First NHL coach to study Soviet coaching methods in Moscow
Fred Shero, Philadelphia, 1974
Shero was not a man to rest on his laurels. He once said, "There's

plenty of room at the top, but not enough to sit down." Only a few days after winning his first Stanley Cup with the Philadelphia Flyers in May 1974, Freddie the Fog flew to Moscow to attend a three-week course on sport and physical education taught by legendary Soviet hockey coach Anatoly Tarasov. Shero believed the Soviets had some terrific ideas. However, few made their way into the Flyers' rough-and-tumble playbook.

Only coach to use the whistle system
Godfrey Matheson, Chicago, 1932–33

Matheson was hired as Blackhawks coach after owner Major Frederic McLaughlin met him on a train. Matheson signalled plays from the bench by blowing a whistle, as though he were directing border collies. One blast meant the player carrying the puck should pass, two meant shoot. Three toots meant fall back and backcheck. It is no real surprise that Matheson had one of the shortest careers of all time: two games, both losses.

Only coach to employ pyramid power
Red Kelly, Toronto, 1976

Having read about the mystical powers associated with Egyptian pyramids, the eccentric Kelly ordered that a large pyramid be suspended from the roof of the Leafs' dressing room during the 1976 playoffs. Smaller pyramids were arranged beneath the Leafs' bench. If players sat beneath the triangles, Kelly insisted, they could tap into psychic energy sources. The players were sceptical, but when captain Darryl Sittler tried it and scored five times in an 8–5 win over the Philadelphia Flyers, many jumped on the bandwagon. Kelly scrapped his pyramid scheme when the Flyers bounced the Leafs out of the playoffs in seven games.

First coach to use videotapes as a teaching tool
Roger Neilson, Toronto, 1977–78

Neilson, who was inducted into the Hall of Fame in 2002, was best known for his perpetually worried expression, unruly hair, loud ties and pioneering use of game film, an innovation that earned him the nickname Captain Video. Neilson began experimenting with video while coaching junior hockey with the Peterborough Petes of the OHA. When he was hired by the Maple Leafs in 1977, he brought his A.V. equipment with him.

First coach to hire an assistant coach
Lynn Patrick, St. Louis, 1967–68

In the first season of expansion, the Blues' GM and head coach hired 34-year-old Scotty Bowman as his assistant. Bowman's job was to handle the defense corps while Patrick oversaw the forwards. After the slumping Blues won only four of their first 16 games, Patrick handed over the reins to Bowman, telling him, "You're ready to coach the team." Patrick was right. Under Bowman's command, St. Louis reached the Cup finals.

First coach to use three goalies, one game
Punch Imlach, Toronto, April 3, 1966

The two-goalie concept had just been introduced (in 1965–66) when Imlach stretched the envelope, using three different net-minders, one in each period, against Detroit in the last game of the season. Johnny Bower played the first period, then left with the "flu," Terry Sawchuk played the second and Bruce Gamble took over for the third period of the 3–3 tie. After the second period, Bower returned to sub as coach, while Imlach moved up to the press box to watch the game from a new vantage point.

First coach fined for assaulting a referee

Tommy Gorman, Chicago, March 14, 1933

Gorman blew a gasket protesting a goal by Bruins forward
Marty Barry in a game at Boston Garden in March 1933. The
Chicago coach leaned over the boards and grabbed referee Bill
Stewart. The two were soon tossing punches. Stewart finally
broke free and ordered Gorman to the dressing room. When
Gorman refused to comply, police were called to escort him
away. The Hawks players left the ice with their coach and
refused to return to finish the game, which Stewart awarded
to the Bruins. Gorman was fined $1,000.

First coach to fine his team for losing to an expansion club

Punch Imlach, Toronto, 1967–68

In a move bound to create hard feelings, Imlach told the players
on his defending Cup-champion team that he would fine them
$100 each for every home-ice loss to an expansion team. The
fines were levied three times during 1967–68, as Toronto lost to
Pittsburgh, Philadelphia and St. Louis.

First brothers to coach against one another in the NHL

Lester and Frank Patrick, NY Rangers vs. Boston, December 16, 1934

The Patricks had coached against one another 20 years earlier in
the Pacific Coast Hockey Association. Their NHL rematch took
place in 1934. Lester was the long-time coach of the Rangers,
while Frank had just been appointed the Bruins' bench boss.
Lester's team won 2–1.

Only trio of brothers to coach in the same season

Brian, Darryl and Dwayne Sutter, 2001–02

The Sutters are believed to be the only trio of brothers to coach
in the same season in North American pro sports. Brian was

coach of the Blackhawks, Darryl ran the Sharks and Dwayne was the pilot for the Panthers. Dwayne feuded with Pavel Bure and didn't last the season.

First father and son to coach in the NHL
Lester and Lynn Patrick
Lester Patrick actually had two sons who coached in the NHL, and both began their careers with the Rangers. Lynn coached the Blueshirts for two years, beginning in 1948–49; Muzz became the team's bench boss in 1953–54.

First European-born-and-trained NHL coach
Alpo Suhonen, Chicago, 2000–01
The 51-year-old Finnish-born Suhonen had 30 years of experience as a head coach in Europe and as an assistant in Winnipeg and Toronto when he joined the Blackhawks in 2000–01. A cultured individual who enjoyed the theatre and classical music, Suhonen didn't get rave reviews in Chicago. He was fired after compiling a 29–45–8 record.

Last player-coach in the NHL
Charlie Burns, Minnesota North Stars, 1969–70
After a dismal 9–13–10 start, Minnesota GM Wren Blair fired himself as the North Stars' coach and appointed veteran centre Burns as player-coach, the last such position in NHL play. It's no wonder. Burns's double duties earned him the lowest single-season goal count (three goals) of his career, and only 10 wins in the 44 games he coached.

Only coach to win a playing trophy
Doug Harvey, NY Rangers, 1961–62
Montreal traded Harvey to New York in exchange for Lou

Fontinato on June 13, 1961. Some believe the deal had more to do with the fact that Canadiens GM Frank Selke had never forgiven Harvey for his prominent role in the founding of the NHL Players' Association than a decline in the All-Star defenseman's skills. In his first year in Manhattan, Harvey served as a player-coach and led the Rangers to their first playoff appearance in four years. Somehow, he also won the Norris Trophy as the NHL's outstanding defenseman.

First coach to win the Jack Adams Trophy
Fred Shero, Philadelphia, 1974
The award for the coach who most contributed to his team's success was first won by the architect of the infamous Broadstreet Bullies. In his third year in the City of Brotherly Love, Shero guided his rowdy Flyers to a Western Division title. Thanks in large part to Shero's coaching, the Flyers upset the Bobby Orr-led Boston Bruins in the Cup finals.

First unanimous choice for the Jack Adams Trophy
Red Berenson, St. Louis, 1981
Berenson proved to be a popular choice as coach. The Blues captain-turned-coach guided St. Louis to second place overall with a 45–18–17 record and 107 points—a 27-point hike from the previous year. The voters were impressed.

First first-year coach to win the Jack Adams Trophy
Bobby Kromm, Detroit, 1978
Kromm won the award as the league's top coach despite compiling a losing record (32–34–14), which gives you an idea of how bad the Red Wings were the year before. Kromm was no

neophyte behind the bench; two years earlier, he coached the Winnipeg Jets to the WHA title.

First coach to win the Jack Adams Trophy in consecutive years

Jacques Demers, Detroit, 1987, 1988
After resuscitating the sad-sack St. Louis Blues, Demers was hired to coach the last-place Wings in 1986–87. In Demers's first season in Motown, Detroit improved by 38 points and made the Conference finals. In recognition, Demers was voted coach of the year. Detroit improved by another 15 points in 1987–88 and again reached the Conference finals. Once more, the voters picked Demers as the league's top bench boss.

First coach to win the Jack Adams Trophy three times

Pat Burns, Montreal, 1989; Toronto, 1993; Boston, 1998
Burns's feat indicates the perils of the profession. Being judged coach of the year in Montreal, Toronto and Boston is impressive, but it also means he was fired three times.

Only coach to win 1,000 games in a career
Scotty Bowman, 1967–68 to 2001–02

For everyone else, 500 wins is the ultimate benchmark. Bowman was directing traffic for the Detroit Red Wings when he won his 1,000th regular-season game February 8, 1997, in Pittsburgh. He would go on to win an NHL-record 1,244 games.

Only coach to win 60 games in a season

Scotty Bowman, Montreal, 1976–77; Detroit, 1995–96
Bowman is the only coach to win 60 games in a single season,

and he did it twice—an amazing 19 years apart. In Montreal, he posted a 60–8–12 record; in Detroit, 62–13–7.

First coach to win 40 or more games in his first five full seasons
Ken Hitchcock, Dallas, 1996–97 to 2000–01

It's hard to believe that NHL teams were initially reluctant to hire Hitchcock because he was overweight. After taking over the Stars midway through 1995–96 (a season in which they finished 22nd of 26 teams), Hitchcock instantly transformed the struggling club into a force, winning 48, 49, 51, 43 and 48 games in his first five full seasons at the helm. A slimmed-down Hitchcock got the boot after one subpar year (36 wins and 90 points), in 2002–03.

First coach to improve his team's point total in five consecutive seasons
Al Arbour, NY Islanders, 1974–75 to 1978–79

After compiling 56 points his first season on Long Island, Arbour guided his team to increases of 88, 101, 106, 111 and 116 points. The steady rise ended in 1979–80, when the Isles recorded 91 points. No one complained, however, when the club went on to win its first of four Stanley Cups. The only coach to match Arbour's mark is Darryl Sutter, who achieved his five-year climb in San Jose between 1997–98 and 2001–02. Sutter didn't get a chance to extend the string to six. He was fired early in the 2002–03 season.

First coach to keep his job despite missing the playoffs for five consecutive seasons
Frank Boucher, NY Rangers, 1942–43 to 1946–47

How long will a team stick with a coach who can't make the play-offs? The record is five years, first set by Boucher in the 1940s. He snapped the string by guiding New York to a fourth-place finish in 1947–48, but then got the hook midway through the 1948–49 season when the Rangers slid back into the cellar. In 2002–03, Barry Trotz duplicated Boucher's survival trick, leading the Nashville Predators to a fifth straight year of futility.

Only coach to lose his last NHL game by 15 goals

Lester Patrick, NY Rangers, January 23, 1944

Patrick's last game behind the bench was a nightmare. The Rangers GM stepped in as an emergency replacement for coach Frank Boucher, who had returned home to Ottawa because his brother had died. The Rangers played like zombies, and were crushed 15–0 by the Detroit Red Wings in the most one-sided rout in NHL history.

Last coach to regularly wear a fedora

Punch Imlach, Toronto, 1979–80

Hats were once standard accessories for NHL coaches. Today, they have vanished like the Edsel. Looking back though, it's hard to imagine Toe Blake without his black fedora or Imlach without a short-brimmed model pushed back on his forehead. (In his later years, Imlach switched from a black hat to a white one. Maybe he was tired of playing the bad guy.) Imlach last wore his chapeau April 11, 1980. The tradition died with him.

CHAPTER 14

Milestone
men

When Maurice Richard set the all-time benchmark for snipers and scored 50 goals during 1944–45's 50-game schedule, he became hockey's first milestone man. The Rocket's goal on March 18, 1945 launched the first of what would become hockey's greatest standards: the 50-goal, 100-point, 500-goal, 1,000-point and 1,000-game plateaus.

First 50-goal season by a rookie
Mike Bossy, NY Islanders, 1977–78
Everyone thought Bossy was too fragile for boiler-plate hockey—
except the Islanders, who drafted him 15th overall. Brilliant
choice. The rookie "toughed it out" and notched 53 goals.

First 50-goal season by a teenager
Wayne Gretzky, Edmonton, 1979–80
Only two players have recorded 50-goal years before turning 20:
Jimmy Carson in 1987–88 and Gretzky, who was just 19 years,
two months old when he potted 51 goals in 1979–80.

First player to score more than 50 goals, one season
Bobby Hull, Chicago, 1965–66
Chicago Stadium shook for seven minutes when 22,000 fans cel-
ebrated Hull's record-breaking marker. Hockey's first 51st goal
came against Cesare Maniago in a 4–2 win over the Rangers on
March 12, 1966. Hull scored 54 goals that season.

First 50-goal player on two different teams, one season
Craig Simpson, Pittsburgh, Edmonton, 1987–88
Mucking between the face-off circles got Simpson his sniper
status and a deal to Edmonton, where Glen Sather had wearied
of Paul Coffey. His midseason trade after 21 games and 13 goals
with Pittsburgh in November 1987 gave Simpson his only 50-goal
season. He potted another 43 goals in 59 games with the Oilers.

First 50-goal player on two different teams, career
Pierre Larouche, Pittsburgh, Montreal, 1974–75 to 1987–88
The expectations were high for Larouche after he scored 53 goals
with Pittsburgh in 1975–76. Unfortunately, his fame is measured
by this one NHL first. After recording 50 goals with Montreal in

1979–80, Lucky Pierre finished out his career in New York, where he almost became the only 50-goal scorer on three different teams after tallying 48 goals in 1983–84.

First 50-goal player traded in the off-season
Jimmy Carson, Los Angeles, August 9, 1988
Trading Carson after his 55-goal year with the Kings in 1987–88 only makes sense when you consider what Los Angeles got in return: Wayne Gretzky.

First non-Canadian-born 50-goal player
Ken Hodge, Boston, April 6, 1974
Born in Birmingham, England, and raised in Ontario, Hodge is an unlikely candidate for this NHL first. He scored 50 goals in 1973–74.

First 50-goal players, by country

PLAYER	TEAM	GOALS	DATE	COUNTRY
Maurice Richard	Montreal	50	03/18/1945	Canada
Jari Kurri	Edmonton	52	03/15/1984	Finland
Bob Carpenter	Washington	53	03/21/1985	USA
Hakan Loob	Calgary	50	04/03/1988	Sweden
Alexander Mogilny	Buffalo	76	02/03/1993	Russia
Jaromir Jagr	Pittsburgh	62	02/23/1996	Czech Republic

First player to score his 50th goal on a penalty shot
Mario Lemieux, Pittsburgh, April 11, 1997
Lemieux still has the best scoring percentage on penalty shots, with six goals in eight attempts, including this 50th in a one-on-one situation against Florida's John Vanbiesbrouck.

Only 50-goal player with a last-place team
Mike Bullard, Pittsburgh, 1983–84
Bullard registered 51 goals with the cellar-dwelling Penguins in 1983–84.

Only player to score his 50th goal three times on his birthday
Phil Esposito, Boston
Three of Esposito's 50th goals were fired on February 20, his birthday: in 1971, 1972 and 1974.

First teammates to score 50th goals in the same game
Mario Lemieux, Kevin Stevens, Pittsburgh, March 21, 1993
Lemieux and Stevens shared a lot of ice time celebrating; each scored their 50th in a 6–4 win against Edmonton.

Last helmetless player to score 50 goals, one season
Al Secord, Chicago, 1982–83
Secord was one of the last of the bareheaded dinosaurs. Playing on Chicago's top line with centre Denis Savard, the burly left-winger rifled in a career-high 54 goals in 1982–83.

First 100-point NHLer, one season
Phil Esposito, Boston, 1968–69
Great playmaking and garbage goals produced a lethal combination, with Esposito counting 126 points in 1968–69.

First 100-point rookie, one season
Peter Stastny, Quebec, 1980–81
This first could arguably go to Wayne Gretzky, but the Great One never had an "official" rookie NHL season. Stastny established his own greatness and scored 109 points in 1980–81.

First 100-point defenseman, one season

Bobby Orr, Boston, 1969–70

Among Orr's many offensive achievements is this little gem: he pegged 120 points in 1969–70.

First 100-point season by a teenager

Wayne Gretzky, Edmonton, 1979–80

One month after turning 19, Gretzky scored his 100th point of 1979–80. He did it in just his 61st career game.

Only 100-point season by a 40-year-old player

Gordie Howe, Detroit, 1968–69

In hockey years, Howe was about as old as the Canadian Shield, but he was rock-solid in scoring, even at age 41. His only 100-point year came in his 23rd season, a year after the NHL doubled to 12 teams.

First 100-point player on two different teams, one season

Jean Ratelle, NY Rangers, Boston, 1975–76

Ratelle scored 15 points in New York before his trade to Boston, where he netted another 90 points.

First 100-point player on two different teams, career
Marcel Dionne, Detroit, Los Angeles, 1971–72 to 1988–89
Dionne recorded eight 100-point seasons, including 121 points with the Red Wings in 1974–75 and 122 points with the Kings in 1976–77.

Only 100-point defenseman on two different teams, career

Paul Coffey, Edmonton, Pittsburgh, 1980–81 to 2000–01

Coffey scored multiple 100-point seasons with Edmonton in

1983–84, 1984–85 and 1985–86, and multiple 100-point seasons with Pittsburgh in 1988–89 and 1989–90.

First 100-point players, by country

PLAYER	TEAM	POINTS	DATE	COUNTRY
Phil Esposito	Boston	126	03/02/1969	Canada
Kent Nilsson	Calgary	131	02/27/1981	Sweden
Peter Stastny	Quebec	109	03/29/1981	Czech Republic
Jari Kurri	Edmonton	104	03/29/1983	Finland
Neal Broten	Minnesota	105	03/26/1986	USA
Alexander Mogilny	Buffalo	127	03/05/1993	Russia

First 100-point player on last-place team, one season

Joe Sakic, Quebec, 1989–90

Sakic was Quebec's one-man show. With no supporting cast, in only his second NHL season, he triumphed over mediocrity to score 102 points on the 21st place Nordiques. Quebec finished an awful 33 points behind 20th-place Vancouver.

First 500-goal player
Maurice Richard, Montreal, October 19, 1957

If greatness comes along only once every generation, then Richard owned his era. After scoring the NHL's first 500th goal, the Montreal Forum's organist played "Il a Gagné Ses Epaulettes" ("He Has Earned His Stripes"). The goal came in Richard's 863rd career game.

First American-born 500-goal player
Joe Mullen, Pittsburgh, March 14, 1997

Mullen earned a permanent place in NHL history after recording his 500th in his 1,052nd game. His celebrated goal, just a few weeks before his retirement, came against Colorado's Patrick Roy.

First European-trained 500-goal player
Jari Kurri, Los Angeles, October 17, 1992

Kurri set many standards in Finland before dazzling the NHL on Wayne Gretzky's line in Edmonton. His 500th was scored into an empty net in his 833rd game.

First 500-goal player more than 40 years old
Johnny Bucyk, Boston, October 30, 1975

Bucyk was 40 years, five months old and in his 21st season when he pegged his 500th goal.

Last 500-goal player who scored all 500 with one team
Steve Yzerman, Detroit, January 17, 1996

If Detroit's Gordie Howe is Mr. Hockey, Yzerman is Mr. Hockeytown. Yzerman scored No. 500 in his 906th game as a Red Wing.

Only father and son to each score 500 goals
Bobby and Brett Hull

Brett claims he subconsciously learned how to be a goal scorer watching his dad "fly up the ice" in Winnipeg, when Bobby was with the WHA Jets. Unfortunately, the same technique didn't work for a lot of other players, who never got anywhere near the 500-goal level. Bobby notched his 500th with Chicago on February 21, 1970; Brett got his 500th with St. Louis on December 22, 1996. The Hulls are the only father and son to both attain 50 goals, 100 points and 1,000 points.

First 1,000-point player

Gordie Howe, Detroit, November 27, 1960

Few scoring feats carry as much honour as the NHL's first 1,000th point. Howe did it in his 938th game.

First 1,000-point defenseman

Denis Potvin, NY Islanders, April 4, 1987

This first eluded a number of great rearguards. Potvin, the cornerstone of the Islanders for four Stanley Cups, was the first 1,000-point D-man.

First American-born 1,000-point player

Joe Mullen, Pittsburgh, February 7, 1995

Mullen is one of the few 1,000-point players to begin his career at age 25. He was the 42nd NHLer to notch 1,000 points.

First European-trained 1,000-point player

Peter Stastny, Quebec, October 19, 1989

Despite playing for the troubled Nordiques through the 1980s, Stastny still beat Jari Kurri—wing man to Wayne Gretzky—to the millennium mark. Both snipers began their NHL careers in 1980–81, but Stastny posted his 1,000th 10 weeks ahead of Kurri's.

First 1,000-point player under age 30

Marcel Dionne, Los Angeles, January 7, 1981

Nicknamed "L'il Beaver" by Gordie Howe, Dionne was just 29 years, five months old when he scored his 1,000th point.

Only player to score 1,000 points in fewer than 500 games

Wayne Gretzky, Edmonton, December 19, 1984

The Great One earned his 1,000th point in just his sixth NHL season. It happened in his 424th game. Runner-up Mario Lemieux needed 513 games.

First three teammates to score 1,000 points, one season
Adam Oates, Phil Housley, Dale Hunter, Washington, 1997–98
The Capitals reached the Cup finals for the first time in franchise history with a veteran team of millennium men. Oates, Housley and Hunter each notched their 1,000th point during the 1997–98 campaign.

First 1,000-game player
Gordie Howe, Detroit, November 26, 1961
Howe was indestructible. He recorded the NHL's first 1,000th game at age 33, in a 4–1 loss to Chicago. Mr. Hockey went on to play 1,767 games over 26 NHL seasons.

First 1,000-game defenseman
Bill Gadsby, Detroit, October 21, 1962
The Wings' lineup in 1962–63 included the two longest-serving warriors in NHL history. Gordie Howe was the leader in games played and Gadsby ranked second.

First American-born 1,000-game player
Gordie Roberts, Boston, December 9, 1992
Roberts was a workhorse, the reliable, unsung rearguard of six NHL teams during a 15-year NHL career. By the time he joined the league in 1979–80, he had already played four years in the rival WHA. His reward came with two Cups in Pittsburgh and, later, recognition for being America's first 1,000-game player.

First European-trained 1,000-game player

Borje Salming, Toronto, January 4, 1988

The first European star in the NHL, Salming was magic for
Toronto during the 1970s and 1980s. Unfortunately, the Maple
Leafs played poorly during the 1980s and Salming wasted his
prime years on a dismal team.

Only 1,000-game player to score fewer than 25 goals, career

Brad Marsh, 1978–79 to 1992–93

Marsh counted on defensive and leadership skills to carry him
through his 1,086 games. In his six-team, 15-year career, he scored
just 23 times—the lowest goal total among all 1,000-game men.

CHAPTER 15

Bragging
rights

Point and goal-scoring champions

receive the Art Ross and Maurice

Richard Trophies. Since the Richard award was

created in 1999, only one player has won both

trophies in the same season. In 2001–02, Calgary's

Jarome Iginla became the first double-scoring

award winner with league highs of 52 goals and

96 points.

First NHL scoring champion

Joe Malone, Montreal, 1917–18

The way he blew through the loop during the league's first season, Malone should have been dubbed Cyclone. He was an unstoppable force with 44 goals and 48 points in the 22-game schedule.

First defenseman to win a scoring championship

Bobby Orr, Boston, 1969–70

Orr may be the greatest NHLer of all time, Wayne Gretzky included. Twice he led the league in scoring: 120 points in 1969–70, 135 points in 1974–75.

First European-trained scoring champion

Jaromir Jagr, Pittsburgh, 1994–95

Just to prove his first crown (in the lockout-shortened 1994–95 season) wasn't a fluke, the Czech winger has since claimed another four titles.

Only rookie scoring champion

Nels Stewart, Montreal Maroons, 1925–26

Stewart joined the NHL at age 23, after five years with the Cleveland Indians of the USA Hockey Association. The Montreal-born rookie won the scoring crown with 42 points in 36 games, and led the league with 34 goals.

First scoring champion to play more than 500 games before winning the title

Marcel Dionne, Los Angeles, 1979–80

Jarome Iginla played 470 games before winning his first scoring crown in 2001–02, but he was a virtual rookie compared to Dionne, who played bridesmaid numerous times to Phil

Esposito, Guy Lafleur and Bobby Orr before finally winning the Art Ross Trophy in 1979–80 with 699 games under his belt.

Only scoring champion to miss more than 20 games

Mario Lemieux, Pittsburgh, 1992–93

It's one of the all-time great sports stories. Only a few hours after his last radiation treatment for Hodgkin's disease, Lemieux was back on the ice. The Penguins had struggled through an 11–11–2 stretch during his 24-game absence and he trailed Buffalo's Pat LaFontaine by 17 points. The comeback was astonishing. Lemieux won the scoring race with 160 points—12 more than LaFontaine. And his team set an NHL record, winning 17 straight games late in the season to finish first overall with 56 wins and 119 points. Half of Pittsburgh's losses occurred in the 24 games that Super Mario missed.

First scoring champion to record 100 points

Phil Esposito, Boston, 1968–69

After Gordie Howe came close with a 95-point effort in 1952–53, the 100-point season seemed a lock. But the NHL had to wait 16 years until Esposito finally punched up triple digits—with 126 points in 1968–69.

Only scoring champion to win the scoring title by more than 75 points

Wayne Gretzky, Edmonton, 1983–84

By 1983–84, Gretzky was routinely beating his second-place opponents by 50 points in the scoring race. That year he upped the ante by finishing with 205 points to Paul Coffey's second-place 126 points, a 79-point margin.

First scoring champion to record more assists than anyone else had points, one season

Bill Cowley, Boston, 1940–41

A top playmaker in the Wayne Gretzky mould, Cowley could see the whole ice. He recorded 45 assists in 1940–41, one point better than five runners-up in the NHL scoring race. The only other NHLer to match Cowley's feat was Gretzky himself, who amassed 125 assists in 1982–83, one point more than runner-up Peter Stastny.

Last scoring champion with less than a point-per-game average

Toe Blake, Montreal, 1938–39

Long before Blake became a coaching god and led Montreal to eight Stanley Cups, he was a scoring champion with the Canadiens. He won the title in 1938–39 with 47 points in the 48-game schedule.

Last scoring champion with more goals than assists
Bobby Hull, Chicago, 1965–66

With the exception of Pavel Bure, the odds of a player winning the NHL scoring derby today with more goals than assists are remote. However, in the Original Six era it was not uncommon. Hull did it twice with the Blackhawks: in 1961–62 and again in 1965–66, when the left-winger notched 54 goals and 43 assists.

Only scoring champion with 200 points

Wayne Gretzky, Edmonton, 1981–82

Until No. 99 came along, recording 200 points in one season wasn't even on the NHL radar. Gretzky racked up a 212-point campaign, his first of four, in 1981–82.

First scoring champion with fewer than 200 shots (minimum 70 games)

Bryan Trottier, NY Islanders, 1978–79

In a remarkable display of economy by a scoring leader, Trottier fired just 187 shots on net and scored 47 times to lead the league with 134 points. On average, scoring champions shoot 322 times to win the crown.

Last scoring champion with fewer than 200 shots

Peter Forsberg, Colorado, 2002–03

The Avalanche centre directed a paltry 166 shots on net, breaking Bryan Trottier's 24-year-old record. Of course, Forsberg also only tallied 29 goals, the lowest total by an Art Ross Trophy winner since Stan Mikita scored 28 in 1964–65.

Last scoring champion from a last-place team

Max Bentley, Chicago, 1946–47

Chicago may have finished in the cellar but it had Bentley, the centerpiece of its famed Pony Line and trade bait in a seven-player swap that sent the slick centre to Toronto after his 29–43–72 career year in 1946–47.

Last player to lose the scoring title based on the most-goals-scored rule

Eric Lindros, Philadelphia, 1994–95

If two players finish tied for the scoring lead, the player with the most goals gets the nod as winner. Only three players have lost a scoring title because of the rule: Andy Bathgate in 1961–62, Wayne Gretzky in 1979–80, and Lindros, who scored 29 goals and 70 points but lost to Jaromir Jagr's 32 goals and 70 points.

First scoring champion with a minus in plus-minus totals
Stan Mikita, Chicago, 1967–68

Others may have preceded Mikita, who was a minus-3 in the first year that the NHL tabulated plus-minus totals, but without hard numbers there is no way of knowing. Only one other scoring champ since has dipped into the minus zone: Wayne Gretzky with a minus-25 in 1993–94.

Only scoring champion with more than 150 penalty minutes
Stan Mikita, Chicago, 1964–65

Until his mid-career morph from Mr. Nasty to Mr. Nice, Mikita was a penalty magnet. His back-to-back scoring titles include the two highest penalty totals ever by a scoring leader: 154 minutes in 1964–65 and 146 minutes in 1963–64. When Mikita won consecutive scoring titles again in 1966–67 and 1967–68, he posted record-lows of 12 and 14 minutes respectively.

Only teammates to finish one-two in the scoring race five times
Phil Esposito and Bobby Orr, Boston, 1969–70, 1970–71, 1971–72, 1973–74, 1974–75

Orr and Esposito were in a league of their own, trading off first and second place in scoring on five occasions. The other great combos of Gretzky-Kurri, Hull-Mikita and Howe-Lindsay couldn't manage it more than twice.

Only players to finish runner-up in the scoring race five times
Maurice Richard, Montreal, 1944–45, 1946–47, 1950–51, 1953–54, 1954–55
Cy Denneny, Ottawa, 1917–18, 1921–22, 1922–23, 1924–25, 1925–26

First brothers to win the scoring championship
Max and Doug Bentley
Just two sets of brothers have captured scoring titles: Charlie and Roy Conacher and the Bentleys, who did it first: Doug in 1942–43, and Max in 1945–46 and 1946–47. Although Charlie Conacher won his first title in 1933–34, it took brother Roy until 1948–49, two years after the Bentleys set the mark.

First brothers to win goal-scoring titles
Charlie and Roy Conacher
Other great brother acts (such as the Bentleys and Richards) have graced the scoresheets, but the Conachers stand alone among siblings as goal-scoring leaders. Charlie netted five titles during the 1930s, and Roy had one in 1938–39.

First goal-scoring champions, by country

PLAYER	TEAM	GOALS	SEASON	COUNTRY
Joe Malone	Montreal	44	1917–18	Canada
Jari Kurri	Edmonton	68	1985–86	Finland
Alex Mogilny	Buffalo	76	1992–93	Russia
Peter Bondra	Washington	34	1994–95	Slovakia
Keith Tkachuk	Phoenix	52	1996–97	USA
Milan Hejduk	Colorado	50	2002–03	Czech Republic

Only goal-scoring leader with more than 70 goals and less than 10 power-play goals
Wayne Gretzky, Edmonton, 1984–85
Although it doesn't seem humanly possible, Gretzky managed to notch 73 goals despite getting only eight on the power play. In

1984–85, he was more of a threat on the penalty kill. He scored 11 times with the Oilers shorthanded.

First goal-scoring leader with a 35-goal margin
Brett Hull, St. Louis, 1990–91
Hull left the competition eating his dust in 1990–91, when he netted 86 goals to Steve Yzerman and Theoren Fleury's 51.

Last scoring leader with fewer than 250 shots
Milan Hedjuk, Colorado, 2002–03
Hedjuk's 50 goals on a minuscule 244 shots represent the kind of finesse-cycling game Europeans have become known for. Teamed with Alex Tanguay and Peter Forsberg of the Avalanche's AMP Line, Hedjuk connected on 20.5 per cent of his shots on net. The last player to do it prior to Hedjuk was Jari Kurri, who notched 68 goals on 236 shots in 1985–86.

First goal-scoring leader with 200 penalty minutes
Keith Tkachuk, Phoenix, 1996–97
In this category, Tkachuk stands (and hits) in a league of his own. While other goal-scoring leaders with high penalty-minute counts come in at a 3:1 box-time-to-goals ratio, Tkachuk posted a nasty 4:1 ratio, averaging four penalty minutes for every goal (228 minutes and 52 goals) in 1996–97.

CHAPTER 16

The trophy hunters

Bobby Orr was the first player to win four major individual NHL trophies in one season. No. 4 bagged his historic foursome in 1970 with the Art Ross, Hart, Norris and Conn Smythe Trophies. Of course, Orr saved the best for last when he sipped champagne from the ultimate trophy: the Stanley Cup.

First player to win 30 or more NHL trophies

Wayne Gretzky, 1979–80 to 1998–99

During his stellar career, Gretzky cut a wide swath through the record books. His grip on major NHL awards was unyielding for more than a decade. He won an amazing 32 awards, including 10 Art Ross Trophies, nine Hart Trophies, five Lady Byng Trophies, five Lester B. Pearson Awards, two Conn Smythe Trophies and the Patrick Trophy.

First player to win eight consecutive NHL trophies

Bobby Orr, 1966–67 to 1978–79

Only Orr and Wayne Gretzky amassed eight trophies in a row. Orr won the Norris as top defenseman every season from 1967–68 to 1974–75; Gretzky was named MVP every season from 1979–80 to 1986–87.

Last player to win seven different individual NHL trophies

Mario Lemieux, 1984–85 to 2002–03

Bobby Orr was the first title-holder of seven different trophies, claiming his last, the Patrick, in 1979. But the most recent player to win seven is Lemieux, who has copped the Calder, Art Ross, Conn Smythe, Hart, Masterton, Pearson and Patrick.

First family to donate an NHL trophy

The Hart family, Montreal, 1923

Hockey's first individual award, the Hart Trophy, was introduced in 1923–24 when Dr. David Hart, father of Canadiens coach Cecil Hart, dedicated the trophy to the NHL's most valuable player. The first recipient was Ottawa's Frank Nighbor.

First unanimous choice in Hart Trophy voting

Wayne Gretzky, Edmonton, 1982

This is one of the more surprising firsts in hockey, considering the dominance of earlier MVP greats such as Bobby Orr and Gordie Howe. On the strength of his record-setting 92-goal year, Gretzky received 65 of a possible 65 first-place votes.

First player to win the Hart Trophy by one vote

Chris Pronger, St. Louis, 2000

In the closest MVP race ever, Pronger received 396 votes to edge scoring champion Jaromir Jagr by one ballot. Pronger led the league in plus-minus (plus-52) and ice time (30:14) in 79 games in 1999–2000. He was the first rearguard to be named MVP in 28 years.

First defenseman to win four Hart Trophies

Eddie Shore, Boston, 1933, 1935, 1936, 1938

Mean *and* talented, Shore collected some of his era's highest penalty counts and point totals by a blueliner. His patented end-to-end rushes literally knocked players off their feet. As dominating as Bobby Orr was, with three MVP titles, Shore won four during the 1930s.

First goalie to win two Hart Trophies

Dominik Hasek, Buffalo, 1997, 1998

To date, only six netminders have won the Hart. Until Hasek, no goalie had ever captured it more than once—and none since Jacques Plante in 1962. Hasek's influence went beyond elevating the middle-of-the pack Sabres to Cup contenders, he revolutionized the goalie position with his unorthodox flopping style, and baffled shooters with his contortions and eccentric play.

First player to win the Hart Trophy on a last-place team

Tom Anderson, Brooklyn Americans, 1941–42

Anderson must have scored high on congeniality. Although he was the only defenseman with a top-10 finish in the scoring race, Anderson's Americans allowed the most goals in the league.

Only goalie to win the Hart Trophy on a last-place team

Al Rollins, Chicago, 1953–54

Despite losing a record 47 games with the doormat Blackhawks, Rollins's gallant play between the pipes earned him MVP status. Rollins usually kept Chicago close: the club lost 15 one-goal games. When he sat out, the Hawks faired much worse. In a two-game stretch without Rollins on November 28 and 29, Chicago was trounced 9–0 and 9–4 by Detroit.

Only player with more than 175 scoring points who did not win the Hart Trophy

Mario Lemieux, Pittsburgh, 1988–89

With a formidable 199 points, Lemieux handily won the scoring race by 31 points. But the Hart went to second-place finisher Wayne Gretzky, who, in his first season in Los Angeles, helped the Kings improve 23 points over the previous year.

Only NHL trophy inspired by a player who won the award in its first season

James Norris Trophy, Red Kelly, Detroit, 1954

The children of the late James Norris, owner of the Red Wings, were so inspired by Kelly's play that they donated an annual trophy for the NHL's best defenseman. Fittingly, Kelly was the award's inaugural winner in 1954.

First player to win multiple Norris Trophies

Doug Harvey, Montreal, NY Rangers, 1947–48 to 1968–69

Harvey was the first of the great defensemen to win multiple Norrises—in a collection of seven awards, six of them awarded between 1954–55 and 1960–61 with Montreal, and one in 1961–62 with the Rangers.

Last Norris Trophy winner on two different teams

Chris Chelios, Montreal, Chicago, 1983–84 to 2002–03

Only three players—Doug Harvey, Paul Coffey and Chelios—have won the Norris on different teams. Chelios bagged the trophy in 1989 with Montreal, and in 1993 and 1996 with Chicago.

Only defenseman to score more than 125 points and not win the Norris Trophy

Paul Coffey, Edmonton, 1983–84

Clearly, the voters weren't swayed by flashy offensive numbers. Coffey's 126-point season, second only to Wayne Gretzky, earned him only second place in the Norris voting—behind Washington's Rod Langway, who won the award with a trifling 33 points.

Last Norris Trophy winner with fewer than 30 points

Pierre Pilote, Chicago, 1962–63

Pilote had 26 points—considered a decent total at the time. The arrival of Bobby Orr a few years later would radically alter that perception.

First player to have an NHL award named in his honour

Georges Vezina, Montreal, 1927

Vezina's contribution to the game in its early years as hockey's premiere stand-up goalie can not be underestimated. He was the Canadiens' first goalie, backstopping the team for 15 straight seasons and never missing a game until he was diagnosed with advanced tuberculosis in 1925. Upon his death in 1926, the Canadiens established an annual trophy to recognize the NHL's top netminder.

First goalie to win five consecutive Vezina Trophies
Jacques Plante, 1952–53 to 1972–73
Montreal's tradition of great goalkeepers didn't begin with Plante, but he embodied everything synonymous with stopping pucks. Plante was eccentric and competitive, a loner and a winner, and he nabbed five straight Vezinas from 1956 to 1960.

Last goalie to win three consecutive Vezina Trophies
Dominik Hasek, Buffalo, 1997, 1998, 1999
Hasek proved beyond a doubt that goaltending is the most important position on a team, especially lunch-pail teams such as the Sabres. Hasek carried his club all the way to the finals in 1999 before losing to Dallas. He also won six Vezinas, one short of Jacques Plante's record of seven.

Only Vezina Trophy winner to record a goals-against average above 3.00
Grant Fuhr, Edmonton, 1987–88
In Edmonton's firewagon system, it wasn't how many goals you gave up but how many you got. Steeped in that damn-the-torpedoes mentality, it's no wonder Fuhr recorded a 3.43 GAA. In fact, as an Oiler, Fuhr never posted an average below 3.00.

Only Vezina Trophy winner to record no shutouts
Billy Smith, NY Islanders, 1981–82
The absence of zeroes next to Smith's name didn't matter, considering his rock-solid 32–9–4 record and 2.97 GAA. (The 1981–82

season was the first time that goals-against averages didn't determine Vezina winners.)

Only goalie to win no games after winning the Vezina Trophy
Johnny Mowers, Detroit, 1940–41 to 1946–47

Few players' careers were affected as dramatically by World War II as Mowers's. After his third season with Detroit (which included the Vezina for a 2.47 GAA, league-leading totals in wins and shutouts, a First All-Star team berth and the Stanley Cup), Mowers enlisted in the armed forces. He didn't return to the NHL until 1946–47. Unfortunately, his edge was gone; he played just seven games, racking up six losses and a tie with Detroit.

First goalie tandem to win the Vezina Trophy
Johnny Bower and Terry Sawchuk, Toronto, 1965

When Sawchuk was awarded the trophy (for the league's lowest goals-against average) based on his 36 games to Bower's 34, he insisted his Toronto teammate share the award. The league agreed, and for the first time the Vezina became a joint award.

First NHL trophy kept in perpetuity by its winners
Calder Trophy, 1937 to 1943

From 1937 to his death in 1943, NHL president Frank Calder bought a new trophy each year for the outstanding rookie of the year. The first rookie to keep his Calder was Toronto's Syl Apps, in 1937.

First Calder Trophy winner with less than 25 points (minimum 70 games, excluding goalies)
Kent Douglas, Toronto, 1962–63

Teemu Selanne's 132 points in 1992–93 may lead all Calder winners in point totals, but defenseman Kent Douglas owns hockey's least distinguished season by a rookie of the year: 22 points in a 70-game schedule. Douglas was the first rearguard to win the Calder.

First Calder Trophy winner with fewer than 75 career games
Frank McCool, Toronto, 1944–45 to 1945–46
McCool had a brief but storybook career. Twenty-five years before rookie Ken Dryden delivered a surprise Stanley Cup to Montreal in 1971, McCool came out of nowhere, led the league in shutouts, won the Calder and then staged one of the most brilliant playoff performances by a rookie goalie, recording four shutouts in 13 games to lift his Maple Leafs past both the heavily favoured Canadiens and Red Wings. He retired after his sophomore season in 1945–46, ending a 72-game NHL career.

First rookie with 100 points who did not win the Calder Trophy
Joe Juneau, Boston, 1992–93
Juneau's worst career move might have been his 102-point year in 1992–93. He got none of the attention a 100-point rookie deserved (because of Teemu Selanne's 132 points) but all of the pressure to duplicate that point total, which he has never done.

Last Calder Trophy winner traded midseason
Ed Litzenberger, Montreal to Chicago, 1954–55
Montreal literally gave away promising rookie Ed Litzenberger to help the slumping Blackhawks shore up their franchise. In 29 games with the talent-rich Canadiens, Litzenberger had just 11 points, but in Chicago, as his ice time rose, so too did his stats. He recorded 40 points in 44 games to win the rookie prize.

First Calder Trophy winner who didn't play in the NHL the following season

Gump Worsley, NY Rangers, 1952–53

His dismal 13–29–8 record aside, the Gumper's Calder win in 1953 didn't come with any of the usual perks accorded to the league's best freshman. The next year, Worsley found himself riding buses and backstopping the WHL Vancouver Canucks. The Rangers finally brought him up for good in 1954–55.

First player to win the Stanley Cup before the Calder Trophy

Gaye Stewart, Toronto, 1942 and 1943

Stewart may be one of the Stanley Cup's luckiest winners. Called up from the AHL Hershey Bears, Stewart played one game for Toronto in the 1942 finals and got his name etched on silver. A deft stickhandler, aggressive but clean, he won top rookie honours in 1943 with 47 points in 48 games.

Last teammates voted first and second in Calder voting, one season

Dany Heatley and Ilya Kovalchuk, Atlanta, 2001–02

If history repeats itself, bet on Atlanta to cop a few Stanley Cups with its dynamic duo of Heatley-Kovalchuk. The last three teams to ice 1–2 rookie tandems in Calder voting—Toronto in 1961, Montreal in 1964 and the NY Islanders in 1976—all became dynasties.

First woman to have an NHL award named in her honour

Lady Byng, wife of Baron Byng of Vimy, Canada's 12th governor general

Lady Byng loved hockey so much (though not its unruly fans apparently) that in 1925 she donated a trophy to reward the most gentlemanly player in the game.

First defenseman to win the Lady Byng Trophy

Bill Quackenbush, Detroit, 1948–49

The Lady Byng is not usually high on the to-do list for most blueliners, but instead of intimidation, Quackenbush used discipline and positioning to defend his zone. He was the first rearguard to win the Lady Byng, during a 131-game penalty-free streak from March 1948 to January 1950.

Last defenseman to win the Lady Byng Trophy

Red Kelly, Detroit, 1953–54

It's been a half-century since a rearguard won the Lady Byng. Clearly, the voters (hockey writers) haven't been impressed, even by three-time runner-up Nicklas Lidstrom. In a position not known for gentlemanly conduct, Kelly won the Lady Byng three times: in 1950–51 (24 penalty minutes), 1952–53 (eight minutes) and 1953–54 (18 minutes).

First player to win the Lady Byng Trophy with three different teams

Wayne Gretzky, 1979–80 to 1998–99

No. 99 won the Lady Byng in 1980 with Edmonton, in 1991, 1992 and 1994 with Los Angeles and in 1999 with the NY Rangers. In all of those years, Gretzky's highest penalty total was 34 minutes—in 1991–92.

First player to earn permanent possession of a trophy

Frank Boucher, NY Rangers, 1935

Boucher won seven Lady Byngs between 1927–28 and 1934–35. During that eight-year stretch he played 364 games and logged only 87 penalty minutes. After Boucher claimed the Byng for the seventh time in 1935, the NHL gave him the hardware to keep; a new trophy was donated by Lady Byng.

First NHL trophy donated by a corporation
Conn Smythe Trophy, 1965

Maple Leaf Gardens Ltd. presented the first individual playoff award, the Conn Smythe Trophy, to honour the former coach, manager and president of the Toronto Maple Leafs. Ironically, Jean Béliveau, captain of the hated Habs, was the first winner of the leaf-bedecked trophy.

First European-trained player to win the Conn Smythe Trophy
Nicklas Lidstrom, Detroit, 2002

The argument that Canadian-born players compete harder for the Cup may have some validity. Only one non-Canadian (American Brian Leetch in 1994) had won the Conn Smythe in 36 years until Detroit's classy Swedish defenseman became the first European to have his name inscribed as playoff MVP in 2002.

First player to win the Conn Smythe Trophy in two consecutive years
Bernie Parent, Philadelphia, 1974, 1975

Five NHLers have been named playoff prince twice, but only two in back-to-back years: Mario Lemieux in 1991 and 1992, and Parent, whose stellar goalkeeping led the Flyers to two Stanley Cups.

Only player to win the Conn Smythe Trophy three times
Patrick Roy, 1986 to 2003

St. Patrick has won MVP playoff awards in three different decades: in 1986 and 1993 with Montreal, and in 2001 with Colorado.

Only Conn Smythe Trophy winner to score more goals during the playoffs than during the regular season

Claude Lemieux, New Jersey, 1995

Lemieux established his reputation as a money performer with Montreal in his rookie season, when he notched 10 goals in the playoffs (after scoring just once in the regular season). He repeated this unusual feat twice more in his career. After scoring just six times for New Jersey in the lockout shortened 1994–95 season, he busted loose for 13 goals in the playoffs—tops among all players—and won the Conn Smythe Trophy. Then, after a humdrum 11-goal year with Colorado in 1996–97, he rifled home 13 goals in the postseason to again lead all playoff performers. However, this time his team didn't win the Cup and Lemieux didn't win the Conn Smythe.

First Conn Smythe Trophy winner traded in the off-season

Wayne Gretzky, Edmonton to Los Angeles, 1988

Three playoff MVPs were rudely rewarded by being traded the summer following their Cup heroics: Gretzky in 1988; New Jersey's Claude Lemieux, who was sent to Colorado in 1995, and Detroit's Mike Vernon, packed off to San Jose in 1997.

CHAPTER 17

The tradition
continues

Stanley Cup playoff tradition calls for blood feuds to form, beards to be grown and octopuses to be thrown. The custom of each player on the winning team spending 24 hours with the Cup is a more recent tradition. The first club to enjoy private time with Stanley was the New Jersey Devils, in 1995.

First player to take the Cup for a victory skate
Ted Lindsay, Detroit, April 23, 1950

When Detroit won at home in 1950, Lindsay began a new playoff tradition. Upon being handed the Cup by captain Sid Abel, he defiantly thrust it toward the Olympia rafters then skated along the boards so everyone could see it up close. "I knew who paid our salaries. It wasn't the owners; it was the people," Lindsay later explained. "This is what we dream about, maybe from the time we're born—to be recognized as the best in the world. I just wanted to share it with the fans."

First victorious captain to hand the Cup to a team-mate in a wheelchair
Steve Yzerman, Detroit, June 16, 1998

It was a mesmerizing moment: Yzerman accepting the Cup and then gently placing the gleaming trophy in the lap of wheelchair-bound teammate Vladimir Konstantinov. Just a few days after Detroit's Cup victory the year before, Konstantinov was involved in a car accident that damaged his brain. Yet, crippled as he was, there was no mistaking Konstantinov's smile when Yzerman put the trophy in his hands. The Wings needed 16 playoff victories to claim the Cup, and they won it June 16, 1998. Guess what? Konstantinov wore No. 16.

First Cup-winning player to say, "I'm going to Disneyland!"
Al MacInnis, Calgary, 1989

Jean Béliveau would never have stuck his face in a TV camera lens and shouted, "I'm going to Disneyland!" Today's champions don't mind. MacInnis clearly liked the money he was paid to become the first Stanley Cup winner to participate in the What's Next ad campaign for the Disney Corporation. The long-running ads, which began in 1987 when Super Bowl MVP Phil Simms uttered the now-famous catch-phrase, have featured more than 30 football, baseball and basketball stars; yacht captains; figure skaters, and Miss Americas.

First team to receive individual Cup rings

Montreal AAA, 1893

Championship rings were not always a reward for Stanley Cup winners: watches, lapel pins and cash were often customary in earlier times. But the very first Cup champions did receive rings. Each player on the Montreal AAA was given a gold ring, a hockey tradition that was revived by the Toronto dynasty teams of the 1940s.

First player to have his Cup ring taken into space

Bobby Orr, June 1996

One of Orr's game-worn Boston Bruins jerseys and one of his two Stanley Cup rings were among the mementoes that blasted off with Canadian astronaut Robert Thirsk on the space shuttle *Columbia* in June 1996. Although the two men had never met, Thirsk admitted that Orr has always been his hero. He personally called the hockey legend to ask if he could fly something of his into orbit, assuming that the player's choice would be something of little value. He was amazed when a package arrived in the mail bearing Orr's diamond-studded 1970 Cup ring with the famous No. 4 engraved on it.

First octopus thrown on the ice

Detroit Olympia, April 15, 1952

Detroit's weird octopus-tossing ritual began when Wings fans Jerry and Pete Cusimano pitched one of the creatures from the stands during Game 4 of the 1952 Cup finals against Montreal.

In the six-team era, teams could win the Stanley Cup in eight straight, and the Cusimano brothers figured the eight-tentacled creature was a natural as a good-luck charm. The Wings wrapped up the Cup that night with a 3–0 win—the first team to capture the Cup in the minimum number of required games (eight).

First team to employ towel power
Vancouver Canucks, April 29, 1982

It was late in the third period of Game 2 of the Conference finals at Chicago Stadium, and referee Bob Myers had given Vancouver a series of questionable penalties to tilt the game in Chicago's favour. Suddenly, Canucks coach Roger Neilson put a white towel on the end of a stick and raised it aloft in mock surrender. His move was copied by other Vancouver players until the bench looked like a laundry line. When the club returned home for Game 3, frenzied fans waved thousands of white towels, prompting Neilson to say that he wished he owned the concession. The inspired Canucks stunned Chicago in five.

First time Kate Smith sang "God Bless America" in person at a Philadelphia Flyers playoff game
Boston vs. Philadelphia, May 19, 1974

Smith's stirring recording of "God Bless America" was a huge hit in 1939. Thirty-five years later, the Flyers used it as inspiration to win their first Cup. Smith was chauffeured from her New York City home to the Philadelphia Spectrum to sing the song before Game 6 of the finals against Boston. Bruins stars Bobby Orr and Phil Esposito presented Smith with a bouquet of roses in an attempt to monkey with her mojo. It didn't work. The Flyers won 1–0 and Philadelphia celebrated.

First Cup-winning team invited to the White House

Pittsburgh Penguins, June 24, 1991

Pittsburgh's 1991 Cup triumph was the first by an American franchise since the New York Islanders' victory in 1983, which may explain why the club was the first NHL team invited to the White House. The Pens met president George Bush Sr.

Last team to not receive the Cup after winning it

Toronto Maple Leafs, 1947

Although the Leafs led their finals series with Montreal three games to two, the Cup was left behind in Montreal on orders from Leafs GM Conn Smythe when the teams returned to Toronto for Game 6. Smythe figured bringing the trophy along might make his team overconfident. As a result, when the Leafs won 2–1, there was no Cup to raise.

First woman to have her name engraved on the Cup

Marguerite Norris, Detroit, 1954

Norris became the league's first female executive upon the death of her father, James Norris, and served as president of the Red Wings when Detroit won the title in 1954 and 1955. She was presented with the Cup by NHL president Clarence Campbell on-ice at Detroit's Olympia, April 16, 1954.

First player to have his name spelled four different ways on the Cup

Jacques Plante, Montreal, 1956, 1957, 1958, 1959

Despite backstopping the Canadiens every year during their record five consecutive championships from 1956 to 1960, Plante had four versions of his name appear on the Cup. In 1956, it was J. Plante; in 1957, Jacques Plante; in 1958, Jac Plante; in 1959, Jacq Plante; and in 1960, Jacques Plante.

First person to have his name removed from the Cup
Basil Pocklington, 1984

Appearing on the Cup below the names of the 1984 Edmonton Oilers and owner Peter Pocklington are 16 small Xs, put there to cover the name of Basil Pocklington, the owner's father. Pocklington senior's name certainly didn't belong there, as he had no official position with the team. How did it happen? Some contend the engraver was mistakenly given the list of recipients of miniature Cup trophies instead of the official names list. Others say Pocklington tried to pull a fast one.

First NHL team to have its name misspelled on the Cup
Toronto Maple Leafs, 1963

How can you tell the NHL's engraver was from Montreal? Maybe the first clue was when the 1963 champion Leafs somehow ended up as "Leaes" on the Cup. It wasn't the only typo, though. There was also the "Bqstqn" Bruins in 1971 and the New York "Illanders" in 1981.

First team to take the Cup on the *David Letterman* show
NY Islanders, May 19, 1983

In what has since become a must-do for New York Cup-winners, Denis Potvin, Bryan Trottier and a few other Islanders brought the trophy on the *Letterman* show two days after winning their fourth straight championship. After kibbutzing with the gap-toothed host, they left the Cup sitting in the second guest chair, where it remained as the night's showbiz types came and went.

First player whose child mistook the Cup for a toilet bowl
Red Kelly, Toronto, 1964

Because Kelly, a member of the Canadian parliament, had to fly to Ottawa the day after Toronto won the Cup in 1964 and missed the team celebration, owner Harold Ballard had the Cup sent to the Kelly home later with a photographer. Kelly's infant son, Conn, was photographed sitting in the silver bowl. Conn found the moment stimulating. "He did the whole load in the Cup. He did everything," Kelly told reporter Kevin Allen. "That's why our family always laughs when we see players drinking champagne from the Cup."

First player to "steal" the Cup

Guy Lafleur, Montreal, 1979

Lafleur caused some tense moments for the Canadiens' vice-president of public relations Claude Mouton when he secretly "borrowed" the Cup from the trunk of Mouton's car and drove to his parents home in Thurso, Quebec. Lafleur placed the Cup on his front lawn, then watched as hundreds of excited locals paraded past. After a day of photo-taking, Lafleur returned the trophy to the team and the panicked Mouton.

First player to sleep with the Cup

Bryan Trottier, NY Islanders, 1980

The 1980 Conn Smythe Trophy winner managed to arrange a *ménage à trois* with Lord Stanley and his wife. "I wanted to wake up and find it right beside me. I didn't want to just dream of this happening," Trottier explained.

First player to feed his dog out of the Cup

Clark Gillies, NY Islanders, 1980

After the Islanders won their first Cup in 1980, the big winger let his German shepherd, Hombre, eat Ken-L-Ration out of the silver bowl. Asked why, Gillies replied, "Why not? He's a nice dog."

First player to take the Cup to a strip club

Mark Messier, Edmonton, 1990

The Oilers captain took the Cup to the Forum Inn, a strip joint near Edmonton's Northlands Coliseum, and encouraged the peelers to get up close and personal with his lordship.

First player to feed a horse out of the Cup

Ed Olcyzk, NY Rangers, 1994

Thoroughbred fancier Olcyzk took the Cup to the Belmont Park racetrack and let 1994 Kentucky Derby winner Go for Gin use it as a feed bag. At least, that's how the story was reported in the papers. Olcyzk has always insisted he never let the horse actually eat out of the Cup.

First player to have his child baptized in the Cup

Sylvain Lefebvre, Colorado, 1996

The Avalanche defenseman took the Holy Grail angle to a new level, and had his baby daughter baptized in it.

First player to travel with the Cup on a dogsled
Scott Gomez, New Jersey, 2000

Gomez may have Hispanic heritage, but he was born and raised in Anchorage, Alaska. He rode with the Cup into his hometown behind a team of huskies in 2000.

First player to take the Cup to Europe

Peter Forsberg, Colorado, 1996

The Cup made its first trans-Atlantic crossing when Forsberg travelled with the trophy to his hometown of Ornskoldsvik, in northern Sweden, to show it off to the locals.

First players to take the Cup to Moscow's Red Square

Igor Larionov, Slava Fetisov, Slava Kozlov, Detroit, 1997

It makes sense that players from a Red Wings team would be the first to escort the Cup to Russia. Larionov, Fetisov and Kozlov paraded around Moscow's Red Square with the Cup, then posed for photos outside Lenin's tomb.

First player to take the Cup to Asia

Pavel Datsyuk, Detroit, 2002

The Motown rookie took hockey's holy relic to Yekaterinburg, the former city of the Russian czars in the Ural mountains, and placed it on the border between Europe and Asia.

First players to win 10 Stanley Cups

Jean Béliveau and Henri Richard, Montreal, 1971

Big Jean and the Pocket Rocket both won their 10th Cups during the Canadiens' surprise championship of 1971. However, Richard stuck around to capture a record 11th Cup in 1973. Yvan Cournoyer also captured 10 between 1965 and 1979.

Only brothers to win 19 Cups

Maurice and Henri Richard, Montreal

Between them, the Rocket and the Pocket Rocket won more Cups than any other NHL franchise. Way more. Toronto is second to Montreal, with 13.

Only players to appear in 10 consecutive finals

Bernie Geoffrion, Doug Harvey, Tom Johnson, Bert Olmstead, 1951 to 1960

It is a testament to the Canadiens' incredible staying power that Geoffrion, Harvey and Johnson all appeared in 10 straight finals wearing Hab colours from 1951 to 1960. Olmstead played in eight

in a row with Montreal, then two more with Toronto—the
Canadiens' opponents in the 1959 and 1960 finals.

First player to appear in 200 playoff games

Larry Robinson, 1973 to 1992

Robinson became the NHL's first 200-playoff-game man May 19,
1989, when Montreal beat Calgary 4–3 in double overtime to
take a 2–1 lead in the Cup finals. But that was the last celebrating the Canadiens or Robinson would do together. The Habs lost
the next three and the Cup to the Flames. Two months later,
after 17 seasons and 203 playoff games with Montreal, Robinson
signed as a free agent with Los Angeles.

First player to appear in more than 200 playoff games before winning the Cup

Ray Bourque, 1980 to 2001

The gifted blueliner played his 200th playoff game May 4, 2000,
in Colorado's 1–0 loss to Los Angeles. One month later, on June 9,
Bourque's long wait ended as the Avalanche claimed the Cup. It
was his 214th playoff game and his 21st and final season.

First player to wait 15 years between Cups

Chris Chelios, Montreal 1986, Detroit 2002

When Chelios won with Detroit in 2002, it marked his first Cup
since 1986 with Montreal. That 15-year gap eclipsed the record
for longest span between Cups set by Mickey MacKay, who won
in 1915 with the Vancouver Millionaires and then again 14 years
later, in 1929, with the Boston Bruins.

First NHLer to win the Cup with three different teams

Gord Pettinger, NY Rangers, Detroit, Boston

Pettinger won the Cup with every NHL team that signed him.

Born in England, he played junior with the Regina Pats before winning the Cup with New York in 1933, Detroit in 1936 and 1937 and Boston in 1939—more Cups than any other player won during the 1930s. Only five NHLers have equalled his mark: Larry Hillman and Al Arbour (the only other Cup-winning players with three Original Six teams), and Claude Lemieux, Mike Keane and Joe Nieuwendyk.

First player to appear in 20 playoffs
Gordie Howe, Detroit (19), Hartford (1), 1947 to 1980
Mr. Hockey reached the 20-year plateau with the Hartford Whalers in 1980, his last NHL season.

First player to appear in 20 consecutive playoffs
Larry Robinson, Montreal (17), Los Angeles (3), 1973 to 1992
The Big Bird never missed the playoffs in a 20-year NHL career. That says something about Robinson's longevity and excellence.

Only 50-year-old to appear in the playoffs
Gordie Howe, Hartford, 1980
We don't forsee anyone else joining Howe in this club. The ageless wonder was 52 when he suited up for his last playoff series against Montreal in 1980. Think about it. Howe was 24 years older than Canadiens veteran Guy Lafleur.

First American-born NHLer to win the Cup
Harry Mummery, Toronto Arenas, 1918
The Chicago-born defenseman was the lone non-Canadian on the NHL's first Cup-winner, the Toronto Arenas. Mummery scored a goal during the Eastern playoffs and posted six assists during the

finals to reap two more firsts: first non-Canadian to score a goal in the playoffs and the first to notch a point in the Cup finals.

First European-trained players to win the Cup
Stefan Persson and Anders Kallur, NY Islanders, 1980
It wasn't until 1980 that a European mercenary had his name engraved on hockey's highest award. Persson and Kallur, both from Sweden, were members of all four Islanders championship teams between 1980 and 1983.

Only player to captain five Cup champions
Jean Béliveau, Montreal, 1965 to 1971
"Big Béliveau," as announcer Danny Gallivan always called him, captained the Canadiens to championships in 1965, 1966, 1968, 1969 and 1971.

First player to captain two different teams to Cups
Mark Messier, Edmonton, 1990; New York, 1994
If Messier is remembered for any one quality, it is his fierce leadership. He is the first NHLer to captain two Cup winners: the Oilers in 1990 and the Rangers in 1994.

First Cup-winning captain traded the following season
Sid Abel, Detroit, 1952
Three months after Detroit won the Cup in 1952, Abel was traded to Chicago (for cash), where he became playing-coach for the Blackhawks. The favour was returned in 1961 when Eddie Litzenberger, captain of Chicago's Cup-winners in 1961, was sent to Detroit. Only one other Cup captain was traded the next season: Wayne Gretzky, from Edmonton to Los Angeles, in 1988.

First player to captain a Cup-winner and an Olympic champion

Dunc Munro, Canada, 1924; Montreal Maroons, 1926

Six months after Munro captained Canada to its first Olympic gold medal in 1924, he was signed as a free agent by the Maroons, who won their first Cup under his captaincy in 1926.

First player to win a Cup and an Olympic gold medal in the same season

Ken Morrow, NY Islanders, 1980

The bearded D-man from Flint, Michigan, won Olympic gold with the U.S. national team at Lake Placid in February, then joined the Isles and drank champagne from Lord Stanley's silver mug in May.

First player suspended during a Cup finals

Jiri Fischer, Detroit, 2002

It's tough to get suspended in a Cup final. In a century of play, no one had done it until Fischer got a one-game sentence for cross-checking Carolina's Tommy Westlund in the face. Fischer's absence in the series-ending Game 5 cleared the way for defenseman Jiri Slegr, who had suited up only eight times with the Wings during the regular season. His guest appearance allowed him to get his name on the Cup for the first—and quite probably the last—time in his career.

Last pair of brothers to meet as opponents in a Cup finals

Rob and Scott Niedermayer, 2003

When Rob of the Anaheim Mighty Ducks met Scott of the New Jersey Devils in the 2003 finals, they erased a playoff mark that had lasted 57 years. Previously, the last two brothers to go head-to-head in a showdown series were the Reardons: Montreal's Ken and Boston's Terry, in 1946.

First playoff game played in June

Pittsburgh vs. Chicago, June 1, 1992

Even the rapidity with which the Penguins dispatched their
opponents in 1992 couldn't avert the NHL's first June playoff date. The Pens completed the postseason by winning a
record 11 straight games, edging the Blackhawks 6–5 to claim
the Cup.

Last year the Cup was not awarded

1919

Tied at two wins apiece, the finals between the Montreal
Canadiens and the Seattle Metropolitans were cancelled due to
a Spanish influenza epidemic. By this point, several players had
contracted the illness. Canadiens defenseman Joe Hall never left
the hospital. He died of pneumonia April 5, 1919.

Last Cup finals with a Canadian-based team

NY Rangers vs. Vancouver, 1994

At one time it was considered a novelty to have an all-American
Cup finals. Not anymore. Today, it's traditionally the hockey
teams from the Great White North that have to watch the action
from the sidelines. With just six Canadian clubs remaining in
the 30-team league, the odds of that scenario changing are not
good. Although the Ottawa Senators came close in 2003, the last
Canadian team to reach the Cup finals was Vancouver in 1994.
The Canucks were defeated by the Rangers in seven games.

CHAPTER 18

Sniper
fire

If any sniper can fire off words as fast as pucks, it's Brett Hull. In 1999, with one illegal skate inside Dominik Hasek's crease, Hull became the last player to date to score a disputed Cup-winning goal. Later, Hull said: "If it wasn't a real goal, wait till they see my ring."

First brothers to score Cup-winning goals
Corbett and Cy Denneny, 1918, 1927

The Dennenys were the first brothers to win the Cup and the first brother duo to snare Cup-winning goals. Corbett notched the first NHL Cup-clincher in history with Toronto in 1918; Cy bagged his in 1927 with Ottawa.

First defenseman to score a Cup-winning goal
Babe Pratt, Toronto, 1945

Of the half-dozen defensemen to nail Cup-winners, Pratt's goal was one of the most dramatic. He scored at 12:14 of the third period of Game 7 against Detroit to break a 1–1 tie. The fact that Pratt scored was not an unexpected event. He notched 18 goals in the season and was the Leafs' fourth-highest scorer, with 41 points.

Last player to score a Cup-winning goal in his final game
Jacques Lemaire, Montreal, 1979

Overshadowed and underrated—that was Lemaire's status on the talent-laden Canadiens of the 1970s. An excellent two-way centre, he never fell below 20 goals during his entire career. He also won eight Cups in Montreal, two of which were clinched on his goals: in 1977 and 1979. He retired following his second Cup-winner.

Only players to score Cup-winning goals in a Game 7 overtime
Pete Babando, Detroit, 1950
Tony Leswick, Detroit, 1954

Remarkably, both players were Red Wings. Leswick's goal beat the Canadiens in 1954. Babando's goal beat the Rangers in 1950.

First player to score six overtime goals, career

Maurice Richard, 1943 to 1960

Sure, the Canadiens won a lot during Richard's era, but the Rocket was a big reason why. He was a demon with the game on the line. Richard nailed single OT winners in 1946, 1952 and 1957, and he popped three in 1951.

Only player to score overtime goals with four different teams

Glenn Anderson, 1981 to 1996

After his time with the Oilers ended in 1991, Anderson became a hired gun. He scored overtime playoff goals for Edmonton, Toronto, the NY Rangers and St. Louis to end with five, second only to Maurice Richard.

First player to score three overtime goals, one playoff year

Mel Hill, Boston, 1939

With the New York Rangers focussed on shutting down Boston's other big guns, Hill emerged from the shadows to steal the spotlight. After counting only 10 goals in the regular season, the rookie right-winger scored the overtime winners in Games 2, 5 and 7, and earned himself the nickname "Sudden Death."

First defenseman to record a playoff hat trick

George Boucher, Ottawa, March 10, 1921

Boucher scored three times in a 5–0 Senators win over Toronto during the 1921 NHL finals. Forty-nine years elapsed before D-man Bobby Orr duplicated the feat, notching three goals in a 5–2 Bruins victory over Montreal on April 11, 1971.

First rookie defenseman to record a hat trick

Andy Delmore, Philadelphia, May 7, 2000

Only 10 rearguards in NHL history have registered three goals in a postseason game, and Delmore is the only rookie to do it. It would be hard to imagine a more unlikely candidate; the unheralded Delmore had scored only two career goals in 29 NHL games. He notched his hat trick in Game 5 of the Eastern Conference semifinals as Philadelphia beat Pittsburgh 6–3.

First defenseman to score a hat trick in a Cup finals

Eric Desjardins, Montreal, June 3, 1993

Desjardins potted the first hat trick by a D-man in a showdown series. His third came at 0:51 of overtime against the Los Angeles Kings.

Only player to record two playoff hat tricks, career

Dino Ciccarelli, 1981 to 1999

Some may be surprised to hear that Ciccarelli scored 608 regular-season goals. He added another 73 in the playoffs, including a record two playoff hat tricks with Detroit: the first on April 29, 1993 against Toronto; the second on May 11, 1995 against Dallas.

First player to record a five-goal game in the playoffs and score all of his team's goals

Maurice Richard, Montreal, March 23, 1944

In playoffs action, five players have posted a five-goal game, but Richard is the only shooter to account for all of his team's goals. The explosion came in Game 2 of the semifinals as Montreal dumped Toronto 5–1.

Last player to record a five-goal game in the playoffs

Mario Lemieux, Pittsburgh, April 25, 1989

In Game 5 of the Patrick Division final, Lemieux lit up the Flyers for five goals and three assists to equal two playoff records: most points in a game and most goals. Pittsburgh won the game 10–7, but lost the series.

First player to score 10 goals in his first postseason

Maurice Richard, Montreal, 1944

If any spectacle forecast the arrival of a scoring star, it was the Rocket's record-shattering 12-goal performance during the 1944 playoffs. In his first NHL postseason, Richard tallied a dozen in nine games and led Montreal to its first Cup in 13 years. The next year he would score 50 in 50.

Only player to score goals in 10 consecutive playoff games

Reggie Leach, Philadelphia, 1976

Ten in a row; 19 for the entire playoffs. Leach was red-hot in 1976. His streak started April 17 in Game 4 of the quarterfinals in Toronto, and ended May 9 in Game 1 of the finals in Montreal. His record 10-game run included 15 goals.

First player to score 35 power-play playoff goals

Mike Bossy, 1978 to 1987

In Bossy's 10-year career, he played 129 playoff games and scored 85 goals—35 of which were on the man-advantage. His record was only surpassed by Brett Hull, in 2002.

Last player to hold career records for most points and penalty minutes in the playoffs

Gordie Howe, Detroit, 1965 to 1968

Howe was the best player of his time. He was also the toughest. During the 1964 semfinals, he posted his 127th playoff point to eclipse Maurice Richard as the career leader, then in 1965 semi-finals, broke Richard's career playoff penalty-minute record of

188. He held both marks until 1969, when John Ferguson passed him in the penalty parade. Two years later, Jean Béliveau replaced Howe as the playoffs point king.

Only player to twice lead the playoffs in scoring with a team that didn't make the finals
Peter Forsberg, Colorado, 1999, 2002

It's not unknown for a player on the losing Cup-finalist team to win the playoff scoring race, but how often has a postseason scoring leader failed to reach the finals? It's rare. It happened in 1929 and 1931, but since then only five playoffs have featured scoring winners eliminated in the semifinals: Bill Goldsworthy, the first player from a post-1967 expansion team to lead the NHL playoffs, in 1968; Phil Esposito in 1969; Doug Gilmour and Bernie Federko in 1986; and Forsberg. The Swede is unique since he did it twice, when Colorado failed to reach the finals in 1999 and 2002. The two years that Colorado qualified for the finals and won the Cup, 1996 and 2001, Forsberg didn't win the playoff scoring race; teammate Joe Sakic did.

Only players to lead playoff scoring with two different teams
Marty Barry, 1928 to 1940
Wayne Gretzky, 1980 to 1999
The Great One claimed five postseason scoring titles with Edmonton, and his sixth and last in 1993 as a member of the Los Angeles Kings. Barry won the scoring derby with Boston in 1930, and with Detroit in 1937.

First player to record 40 points, one playoff year
Wayne Gretzky, Edmonton, 1985
Gretzky shattered his own playoff mark of 38 points, set two

years before, with a superhuman display in 1985. He racked up 47 points on 17 goals and 30 assists in only 18 playoff games—a decent *season*'s work for some players. Gretzky's total remains a playoff record.

First player awarded a penalty shot in the playoffs
Babe Dye, Toronto St. Pats, March 20, 1922

More than a decade before the NHL's first penalty-shot rule was enforced in 1934–35, Lester and Frank Patrick's Pacific Coast Hockey Association introduced its own version, the "free shot" rule. The rule was tested and considered something of a joke during the 1922 Stanley Cup finals, when the Toronto St. Pats and Vancouver Millionaires squared off using PCHA and NHL rules in alternating games. Referee Cooper Smeaton awarded Dye a shot against goalie Hugh Lehman, after the Toronto sharpshooter was tripped by Art Duncan of Vancouver. Dye had to stand 36 feet out from the net and shoot. He fired the puck far over the cage, which produced this observation in the *Globe and Mail:* "Duncan was not penalized, and he can keep on tripping attackers as long as he likes, as it is not likely the Patricks will win any games from the 36-foot mark. It is hard enough to get the puck past the veteran goalkeeper when only a few feet away."

First defenseman awarded a penalty shot in the Cup finals
Virgil Johnson, Chicago, April 13, 1944

Among the seven shooters to take penalty shots in finals history, Johnson is the only defenseman. He was stonewalled by Montreal goaltender Bill Durnan. Johnson wasn't the ideal candidate for the job. During his 75-game career, he netted only one goal.

Last player awarded a penalty shot in the Cup finals
Pavel Bure, Vancouver, June 7, 1994

No player in NHL history has created as many penalty-shot situations for himself as Bure. The Breakaway Kid has gone *mano-a-mano* a record 10 times during his career, including once during the 1994 finals against the New York Rangers' Mike Richter. Bure was blanked, just like each of the six players before him who were awarded penalty shots in the finals.

Only player with a career playoff plus-minus mark above 90
Charlie Huddy, 1981 to 1997

Even the keenest trivia buffs would be hard-pressed to name the player with the highest career plus-minus in the playoffs. You might guess it would be a former member of the high-scoring Edmonton Oilers, but you wouldn't think of Huddy. The steady blueliner compiled a plus-93 in 183 playoff games. That's five more than Jari Kurri, the next highest at 88.

First player to score 100 playoff goals
Wayne Gretzky, May 7, 1993

Although Gretzky was the first to hit the century mark, his accomplishment was anything but assured entering the 1993 postseason. Trailing the Great One's 95 goals was teammate Jari Kurri, with 93. Gretzky recorded his 100th May 7 against Vancouver in the Division finals, just six games before Kurri scored his 100th on May 21 against Toronto in the Conference finals. Gretzky ended his career with 122 playoff goals; Kurri had 106.

CHAPTER 19

Keepers
of the flame

In 1993, Montreal's Patrick Roy

became the first and only netminder

to register 10 overtime victories in one postseason.

Even more remarkable, those 10 sudden-death

wins were recorded in an unbroken string. You

can't lose with that kind of goaltending, and

Montreal didn't, clinching the Cup with a 4–1 win

over the Los Angeles Kings.

First goalie to face 5,000 playoff shots

Patrick Roy, 1986 to 2003

Roy has faced more shots (7,149), given up more goals (584) and made more saves (6,559) than anyone else to step between the pipes in the postseason. It's safe to say he is first with 5,000 shots, 500 goals against and 5,000 saves. He is the king.

First goalie to record 100 playoff wins

Patrick Roy, 1986 to 2003

St. Patrick passed the century plateau April 24, 1999, in Colorado's 3–1 victory against San Jose. Upon his retirement in 2003, Roy's total was 151 wins.

First goalie to record 75 playoff losses

Patrick Roy, 1986 to 2003

Amid his multitude of playoff records, this is Roy's bitter pill. He leads all goalies with 94 playoff losses; his 75th was on May 4, 2001, in Colorado's 1–0 loss to Los Angeles.

First goalie to allow a penalty-shot goal in the playoffs

Terry Sawchuk, Los Angeles, April 9, 1968

Sawchuk gave up the playoff's first penalty-shot goal to Minnesota's Wayne Connelly in a 7–5 loss to the North Stars. Prior to this event, only three penalty shots had been awarded in 50 years of postseason play. All were unsuccessful.

First goalie to face 100 shots, one game (including overtime)

Tiny Thompson, Boston, April 3, 1933

Boston's Tiny Thompson and Toronto's Lorne Chabot staged an epic goaltender's duel in the NHL's second-longest game. Thompson broke the triple-digit barrier for the first and only time in history with 113 saves, while Chabot turned back 93 in the 1–0 Toronto win. The pair combined to stop a record

206 shots during six overtime periods, playing 164 minutes and 46 seconds of shutout hockey.

First goalie to record 20 playoff shutouts
Patrick Roy, 1986 to 2003

Roy is as prolific as Wayne Gretzky, according to the NHL record books. He leads all goalies with 22 shutouts. His 20th came April 23, 2002, in Colorado's 1–0 blanking of Los Angeles.

First goalie to record five shutouts, one playoff year
Dominik Hasek, Detroit, 2002

Hasek blew past a long-standing NHL barrier of four playoff shutouts when he whitewashed Colorado 7–0 on May 31, 2002. Hasek later beat Carolina 3–0 in Game 4 of the finals, to make it a record total of six shutouts. New Jersey's Martin Brodeur upped the record to seven shutouts in 2003.

First goalie to record a shutout in his first playoff game
Lorne Chabot, NY Rangers, April 2, 1927

Chabot became the first rookie to earn a zero in his first playoff game when he blanked Boston in a 0–0 tie during the 1927 semifinals. Ironically, his opponent was the Bruins' Hal Winkler, who four months earlier became the first goalie to notch a shutout in his first regular-season game.

First goalie to record shutouts in his first three playoff wins
Brent Johnson, St. Louis, 2002

In the opening round of the 2002 playoffs, the Blues rookie stoned the Chicago Blackhawks for 207 minutes, recording three straight shutouts. Johnson became the first goalkeeper in 57 years to post three consecutive zeroes in a series, and the first in history to notch goose eggs in his first three postseason wins. No surprise, St. Louis won in five.

Only goalie to record three consecutive shutouts in a Conference finals

Jean-Sebastien Giguere, Anaheim, 2003

Giguere's emergence as a postseason saviour was sudden and un-expected. Displaying perfect technique, the unflappable Mighty Ducks netminder led his club to huge upsets over Detroit and Dallas in the opening two playoff rounds. He continued his heroics against Minnesota in the Western Conference finals, stopping all 98 shots directed his way during the first three games. The Wild finally beat Giguere in the first period of Game 4, snapping his series shutout streak at 213 minutes and 17 seconds, but it was the only puck that got past him as the Ducks won 2–1 to cap the sweep.

Only goalie to record three consecutive shutouts in a Cup finals

Frank McCool, Toronto, 1945

Martin Brodeur of the Devils in 2003 and Clint Benedict of the Maroons in 1926 also posted three zeroes in a Cup finals, but McCool is the only netminder to do it in consecutive games. The rookie blanked Detroit in the first three games of the 1945 finals. The Wings rebounded for three wins, but Toronto took Game 7 and the Cup.

First goalie to appear in 100 playoff games

Turk Broda, Toronto, 1937 to 1952

Broda was one of hockey's best money goalies. A solid regular-season goals-against average of 2.53 turned into a stellar

1.98 average at playoff time. Broda played 101 career postseason games; his 100th, a 1–0 loss to Detroit, on March 27, 1952.

First goalie to appear in 200 playoff games
Patrick Roy, 1986 to 2003

Roy hit the 200-game mark in a 5–1 win against Vancouver on April 18, 2001. The Canucks, Roy's opponent that night, had only played 128 playoff games in their franchise history. The next-closest netminder is Grant Fuhr, with 150. (Ed Belfour has 148.)

First fight between goalies in the playoffs
Turk Broda and Harry Lumley, April 10, 1948

Although it's difficult to confirm, the first two goalies to square off in postseason action were probably Lumley and Broda, who slugged it out during Game 2 of the Detroit–Toronto finals of 1948. Lumley (six foot, 195 pounds), three inches taller and 15 pounds heavier than the stocky Broda (five foot nine, 180 pounds), had the edge in size, but no winner was declared.

First goalie to score a playoff goal
Ron Hextall, Philadelphia, April 11, 1985

Hextall's second career bull's eye—and the first by a masked man in the postseason—was an empty-netter. He flipped the puck the length of the ice into the abandoned cage in an 8–5 win against Washington.

First goalie to record a playoff assist
Johnny Bower, Toronto, March 26, 1963

In Game 1 of the 1963 semifinals against Montreal, Bower kicked out a shot to defenseman Allan Stanley, who hit Bob Pulford

with a pass at centre ice. Pulford scored on the rush, earning
Bower the first assist by a goalie in postseason play.

First goalie to record a playoff assist on an overtime goal
Dominik Hasek, Detroit, May 22, 2002

The Dominator fed a lead pass to Steve Yzerman that was converted
into Fredrik Olausson's goal at 12:44 of the first overtime period, as
Detroit beat Colorado 3–2.

First goalie to win Cups in three different decades
Patrick Roy, 1986 to 2003

Add this little bauble to Roy's war chest of career records.
The butterfly goalie by whom all others are judged won
one Cup during the 1980s (Montreal, 1986), two during
the 1990s (Montreal, 1993 and Colorado, 1996) and one in
2001 (Colorado).

Only goalie to captain a Cup-winner
Charlie Gardiner, Chicago, 1934

Gardiner captained Chicago to its first Stanley Cup in 1934, lim-
iting Detroit to two goals in his team's three victories. In the last
game of the best-of-five final series, Gardiner held off the Wings
and stopped 40 shots before Chicago's Mush March netted the
series winner at 30:05 of overtime.

First goalie tandem named to a Cup champion
Tiny Thompson and Hal Winkler, Boston, 1929

In the era of the one-goalie system, co-crediting netminders
with a championship was unheard of. But the Bruins had a soft

spot for Winkler, who had performed admirably during the 1928 finals before losing to Ottawa. When Thompson replaced Winkler and backstopped Boston to the Cup in 1929, the club listed Winkler as a "sub-goalie," etched his name on the Cup and included him in the official team photo, even though he spent the entire season with the Minneapolis Millers of the American Hockey Association.

First rookie goalies to meet in a Cup finals

Frank McCool and Harry Lumley, April 6, 1945

In the first NHL rookie netminder's duel in finals history, Frank McCool of the Leafs defeated the Red Wings and Harry Lumley 1–0.

First European-born NHL goalie to win the Cup

Andy Aitkenhead, NY Rangers, 1933

Several successful goalies in the NHL's early days hailed from Scotland. Aitkenhead was born in Glasgow, which explains his nickname, the Glasgow Gobbler. A veteran of the Pacific Coast Hockey League, Aitkenhead joined the Rangers in 1932–33 and led them to the Cup in his first NHL campaign. The following year, another Scotsman, Charlie Gardiner, backstopped Chicago to the Cup.

First European-trained goalie to win the Cup

Dominik Hasek, Detroit, 2002

The eccentric Czech with the rubbery limbs had won an Olympic gold medal, the Vezina Trophy, the Hart Trophy and kudos as the best goalie in the world, but Lord Stanley's silverware eluded him until 2001–02 when he joined the star-studded Red Wings. Hasek prevailed under pressure in the playoffs, got his name etched on the Cup and then retired.

Only goalie with no big-league experience to lead an NHL team to the Cup
Earl Robertson, Detroit, 1937
Ken Dryden played only six regular-season games before winning a Cup with Montreal in 1971, but Robertson was even greener: he had his NHL debut in the playoffs. After spending the year with the American Hockey League's Pittsburgh Hornets, Robertson was called up to replace injured starter Normie Smith. He performed like a seasoned vet, blanking the Rangers in the crucial fourth and fifth games of the best-of-five finals.

First goalie involved in three overtime Cup-deciding games
Gerry McNeil, Montreal, 1951, 1953, 1954
Ed Belfour has been there twice, in 1999 and 2000; and so has Gerry Cheevers, in 1970 and 1977. But McNeil lived to tell about three times: losing the Cup in overtime in 1951 and 1954, and winning in 1953. Pretty remarkable for a five-year playoff career.

Only goalie to play for six losing Cup finalists
Glenn Hall, 1953 to 1971
Hall was a six-time loser in the finals with three different teams: Detroit in 1956; Chicago in 1962 and 1965; and St. Louis in 1968, 1969 and 1970. Thankfully, the man they call Mr. Goalie took home the silverware once, in 1961 with Chicago.

Last 40-year goalie to win the Cup
Gump Worsley, Montreal, 1969
The Gumper, who had turned 40 two weeks earlier, was 10 years older than Montreal coach Claude Ruel when he backstopped the Canadiens to a sweep of St. Louis in the 1969 Cup finals. The Blues' goaltending tandem was equally "ancient": Jacques Plante was 40 and Glenn Hall was 37.

CHAPTER 20

Dancing
with destiny

The first and only NHL team to

compile more than 130 regular-

season points and not win the Stanley Cup was the

Detroit Red Wings in 1995–96. As dominant as

Detroit was over six months, the club was not

destined to go all the way. The Colorado Avalanche

snowed the Wings under in the Western

Conference finals.

First NHL dynasty team

Toronto Maple Leafs, 1947, 1948, 1949

After posting first and second finishes and winning back-to-back Cups, the Maple Leafs slumped to fourth in 1948–49. But they rebounded in the playoffs, beating Boston in five games and Detroit in four to capture a third straight championship.

First team to win the Cup with a sub-.500 regular-season record

Chicago Blackhawks, 1937–38

If any American NHL club can be compared to the USA's "Miracle on Ice" team of the 1980 Olympics, it was the 1938 Blackhawks. Long shots at best for a championship, the Hawks slipped into the playoffs with a 14–25–9 record and an unheard of eight U.S.-born players on the roster. Great goaltending and determination won the day. Chicago was stretched to full counts against Montreal and the NY Americans in the early rounds, then defeated Toronto in four games in the best-of-five finals to take the prize. Only one other team has claimed the Cup with a sub-.500 mark: the 1948–49 Maple Leafs.

First team to record more than 120 regular-season points and lose the first playoff round

Boston Bruins, 1970–71

Some other team may eventually match this tumble, but for now the 1971 Bruins are lonely at the top. After running roughshod over the league and compiling 121 points (57–14–7) during the regular season, Boston fell prey to overconfidence and spectacular goaltending by rookie Ken Dryden and lost to the third-place Montreal Canadiens in the first playoff round.

First team to lose four overtime games in a Cup final

Montreal Canadiens, 1951

So close and yet so far. All five games of the 1951 showdown between Montreal and Toronto were decided in overtime; the Canadiens left the ice as losers four times. No other team has suffered this indignity.

Only team to survive eight elimination games, one playoff year

New York Islanders, 1975

They say you have to persevere through adversity to become a champion. If that's true, then New York laid the foundation for its future dynasty in 1975. After dropping Game 2 of the best-of-three preliminary round with the Rangers, the Isles won the series in Game 3. In the quarterfinals they lost three straight to Pittsburgh, before storming back to take the series in seven games. Then, in the semifinals, after falling behind by three games to Philadelphia, they rebounded to win three games with their back to the wall, before taking the fatal bullet in Game 7. It was quite a ride.

First American team to win the Cup

Seattle Metropolitans, 1917

The Metropolitans wore red-white-and-green uniforms with a candy-cane "S" on the chest. They were led to the Cup by Regina-born Jewish scoring star Bernie Morris, who accounted for 14 of Seattle's 23 goals in the four-game final against the Montreal Canadiens, including six in the 9–1 Cup-clincher.

First team to win the Cup with an American coach

Montreal Canadiens, 1924

Yes, the Canadiens. Born in Bourbonnais, Illinois, Leo Dandurand was one of the top sports entrepreneurs of his day.

He bought the Canadiens for $11,000 in 1921 and coached the team to its first Cup as a member of the NHL in 1924.

First American teams to meet in the Cup finals
Boston Bruins vs. New York Rangers, March 28, 1929
The first all-American Cup final was an Eastern seaboard affair. The Bruins swept the best-of-three series by scores of 2–0 and 2–1 to claim their first Cup. It would be 43 years before the Bruins and Rangers would meet again in the finals.

Last non-NHL team to win the Cup
Victoria Cougars, 1925
The Western Canada Hockey League champions downed the NHL champion Montreal Canadiens in the best-of-five final three games to one. The Lester Patrick-coached club was led by future Hall of Famer Frank Fredrickson, who outplayed Montreal superstar Howie Morenz. According to Charles Coleman in his book *The Trail of the Stanley Cup:* "The Cougars were too fast for the Canadiens and skated them dizzy."

Last all-Canadian team to win the Cup
Philadelphia Flyers, 1975
Although most Canadian hockey fans associate the bully-boy Flyers with a distinctly American approach to the game, they were the last team composed entirely of Canadian-born players to claim the Cup.

Only team to win five straight Cup finals
Montreal Canadiens, 1956 to 1960
Capturing five straight Cups ranks right up there with the toughest of hockey accomplishments. Detroit in 1956, Boston in

1957 and 1958, then Toronto in 1959 and 1960. The Canadiens mowed them all down.

Only visiting team to win the Cup at the Montreal Forum
Calgary Flames, 1989

Calgary lassoed its first Cup by doing what no other NHL club had ever done: send Montreal down in flames in front of its hometown fans. Doug Gilmour notched the Cup-winner in a 4–2 victory in Game 6.

Only team to win the Cup in a Game 7 overtime
Detroit Red Wings, 1950, 1954

Detroit is the only team to win the Cup on a series-deciding overtime goal in Game 7. The Red Wings danced the tightrope in 1950, when they won both the semis and finals in overtime in Game 7. Remarkably, they went to the limit again in 1954, defeating Montreal in overtime in Game 7 to bag the trophy.

Last team to win the final game in a playoff series but lose the series
Chicago Blackhawks, March 26, 1936

They say if you win your last playoff game you're a Cup-winner. But not always. Prior to 1936, the NHL often employed a two-game total-goal format to determine series winners. This created some weird scenarios. For example: the New York Americans defeated Chicago 3–0 on March 24, but the Blackhawks battled back in Game 2 with a 5–4 win. Even though Chicago won the last game of the series, the Americans took the series on total goals, 7–5.

Last time an overtime playoff goal resulted in a tie

Chicago Blackhawks vs. Montreal Canadiens, March 25, 1934

This could only have happened prior to 1936, when some play-offs were decided by total-goal counts. After a 3–2 Hawks win March 22, Montreal and Chicago met for their final game three nights later. After 60 minutes, the Canadiens had a 1–0 lead, which tied the series in goals. Chicago scored first in overtime, tying the game 1–1 and winning the series 4–3 on total goals.

First team to win 10 overtime games, one playoff year

Montreal Canadiens, 1993

Eleven of the 20 playoff games that Montreal played in 1993 were decided in OT. The Habs won 10 of them, in large part because goalkeeper Patrick Roy was on fire. The previous record was six overtime victories, set by the 1980 Islanders.

First team with a 10-day layoff between playoff series

Anaheim Mighty Ducks, 2003

After taming the Minnesota Wild in four straight games, the boys from Disney's Magic Kingdom found themselves with time on their hands. The Ducks had to wait 10 days to play their next adversary, the longest span in modern NHL history. Anaheim's break started after its last game against the Wild on May 16 and ended May 27, with its opening match against New Jersey in the finals. The 1966 Montreal Canadiens had the next-longest layoff: nine days.

Last team to play no home games, one series

New York Rangers, 1950

The Rangers and their fans have long suffered from other book-ings at Madison Square Garden at playoff time. In the 1950 finals, the Rangers got bumped by the circus, only to find a carnival-like atmosphere on the road. Toronto's Maple Leaf Gardens subbed as the Rangers' home rink during the series, but only two of the seven games were played there. After the Rangers took a 3–2 series lead, Detroit hosted the last two games. Game 6 should have been played in Toronto, but a strange piece of legislation stipulated that a deciding Cup game could not be played on a neutral rink. A Rangers win in Game 6 would have been a "deciding" result. So Detroit's Olympia became the "home" site for New York; not that it made any difference to the 13,000 screaming Red Wings fans. Leading 4–3 in the third period, the Rangers gave up a goal and then lost in overtime. Then, in Game 7, the Wings beat New York in double-overtime. Blame Barnum and Bailey.

First coach to coach a team 1,000 games without winning the Cup
Billy Reay, Chicago, 1963–64 to 1976–77
Reay coached 1,012 regular-season games in Chicago, leading the Blackhawks to several division titles, a first-place finish overall in 1966–67 and three trips to the Cup finals. Alas, Reay never tasted Lord Stanley's champagne.

First coach since 1967 expansion to take his team to the Conference finals in his first four seasons
Bob Hartley, Colorado, 1999 to 2002
Even this level of success didn't help Hartley from being fired. He was dismissed by Colorado on December 18, 2002, early in his fifth season.

Only coach to win the Cup in each of his first five seasons
Toe Blake, Montreal, 1956 to 1960
No one is likely to match this feat. The Montreal team that Blake took over in 1955–56 was stocked with talent, but even so, winning

Cups in your first five seasons is a mind-boggling feat. Blake's play-off record in those five years was a dominating 40–9.

First coach to win the Cup with the neutral-zone trap
Jacques Lemaire, New Jersey, 1995
Although some credit (or blame) the European teams with developing the neutral-zone trap, it was Lemaire who used the tactic to pilot the underdog New Jersey Devils to a Cup win in 1995. Lemaire's trapping system befuddled Scotty Bowman's favoured Detroit Red Wings in the finals as the Devils swept the series.

First coach to win Cups with three different teams
Scotty Bowman, Montreal, Pittsburgh, Detroit
Bowman is the only coach to manage this tough trifecta. He won four Cups with Montreal (1976, 1977, 1978, 1979), one with Pittsburgh (1992) and three with Detroit (1997, 1998 and 2002). Aside from Bowman, only Dick Irvin and Tommy Gorman have won Cups with two NHL teams.

Only coach to win the Cup with different teams in back-to-back years
Tommy Gorman, Chicago, 1934; Montreal Maroons, 1935
Few general managers could rationalize firing a coach after capturing the Stanley Cup, but the Hawks' Major Frederic McLaughlin blew Gorman out after he won in 1934 with Chicago. Gorman moved to Montreal to take over the reins of the Maroons and led them to the title. In what must have been a sweet moment for Gorman, the Maroons eliminated Chicago in the first round of the playoffs.

First coach to lose three Cup finals with three different teams

Dick Irvin, Chicago, Toronto, Montreal

Irvin was no stranger to Cup finals: he coached in 16 of them. He was also no stranger to going home empty-handed: he lost 12. Irvin came up short with Chicago in 1931, with Toronto in 1933 and then for a third time, with Montreal in 1947.

First ex-coach to get his name on the Cup despite being fired midseason

Robbie Ftorek, New Jersey, 2000

Although he was handed his pink slip with eight games remaining in 1999–2000, Ftorek still got his name etched on the Cup as a coach after Larry Robinson replaced him and led the Devils to the championship.

Only playing-coach to win the Cup

Cy Denneny, Boston, 1929

Considering that this Boston team was managed by the imposing Art Ross, it's debatable how much coaching Denneny actually did. Denneny earned this rare double in the final season of his 12-year career. He skated in 23 of the Bruins' 44 regular-season games and two of their five playoff games.

Last coach to win the Cup and the Jack Adams Trophy in the same season

Scotty Bowman, Montreal, 1977

The NHL's best regular-season coach almost never wins the Cup—at least, according to the voters. It has now been 26 years since a coach picked up both pieces of hardware. In fact, only two coaches, Bowman and Fred Shero (in 1974), have won the Adams in the same year they won the Cup.

ACKNOWLEDGEMENTS

Thanks to the following for the use of reference material:
- *The Official NHL Guide and Record Book,* various years
- *Total Hockey and Total Stanley Cup* by Dan Diamond and Associates, Inc.
- *The Trail of the Stanley Cup* by Charles H. Coleman
- *The NHL Team Guides,* various years
- *The Unofficial Guide to Hockey's Most Unusual Records* by Don Weekes and Kerry Banks
- *Pavel Bure: The Riddle of the Russian Rocket* by Kerry Banks
- *The Rules of Hockey* by James Duplacey
- *Ultimate Hockey* by Glenn Weir, Jeff Chapman and Travis Weir
- *What's the Score?* by Liam McGuire
- *The Hockey News Century of Hockey,* edited by Steve Dryden
- *Kings of Ice* by Andrew Podnieks and others
- *Years of Glory,* edited by Dan Diamond
- *The Best Book of Hockey Facts and Stats* by Dan Weber
- *The Original Six* series by Brian McFarlane
- *The Hockey Trivia* series and *Old-Time Hockey Trivia* series by Don Weekes
- Also, *The Hockey News, hockeydb.ca, faceoff.com, Sports Illustrated* and the *National Post, Globe and Mail, Vancouver Sun* and *Montreal Gazette.*

Thanks to the following for their use of quoted material:
- *The Stick: A History, A Celebration, an Elegy* by Bruce Dowbiggin. Published by Macfarlane Walter and Ross.

- *Boom-Boom, the Life and Times of Bernard Geoffrion* by Bernard Geoffrion and Stan Fischler. Published by McGraw-Hill Ryerson.
- *Sawchuk: The Troubles and Triumphs of the World's Greatest Goalie* by David Dupuis. Published by Stoddart.

The authors gratefully acknowledge the help of everyone at *The Hockey News;* Gary Meagher and Benny Ercolani of the NHL; Phil Pritchard at the Hockey Hall of Fame; the staff at the McLellan-Redpath Library at McGill University; Rob Sanders, Susan Rana and Chris Labonte at Greystone Books; the many hockey writers, broadcast journalists, media and Internet afficionados who have made the game better through their work; Cathy Newton for thumbing through thousands of pages to check the stats; as well as editor Anne Rose, typesetter Tanya Lloyd Kyi and designer Peter Cocking for their patience, dedication and expertise.

PLAYER AND COACH INDEX

A

Abel, Sid, 182, 192
Adams, Jack, 139
Aitkenhead, Andy, 209
Amonte, Tony, 55
Anderson, Glenn, 6, 87, 197
Anderson, Tom, 172
Andreychuk, Dave, 68, 89
Apps, Syl Sr., 69, 118, 175
Apps, Syl Jr., 69
Arbour, Al, 32, 149, 191
Arnason, Chuck, 56
Astrom, Hardy, 106

B

Babando, Pete, 196
Bailey, Ace, 27, 33
Barry, Marty, 145, 200
Bathgate, Andy, viii, 26, 28, 165
Bauer, Bobby, 69
Beaton, Frank, 112

Belfour, Ed, 207, 210
Béliveau, Jean, viii, 2, 7, 16, 44, 84, 124, 179, 182, 189, 192, 200
Bellows, Brian, 52
Benedict, Clint, 28, 48, 55, 61, 105, 206
Bentley, Reg, 45–46
Bentley, Doug, 45–46, 70, 85, 166
Bentley, Max, 45–46, 70, 165–166
Berenson, Red, 147
Bergman, Gary, 27
Berry, Bob, 69
Berube, Craig, 116
Bibeault, Paul, 6, 31
Bierk, Zac, 100
Biron, Martin, 32
Bladon, Tom, 54, 65
Blair, Andy, 9, 53
Blake, Toe, 43, 70, 107, 150, 164, 217
Blinco, Russ, 54

Boesch, Garth, 53

Bombardir, Brad, 46

Bondra, Peter, 167

Bossy, Mike, 67, 76, 152, 199

Boucher, Brian, 103

Boucher, Frank, 149–150, 178

Boucher, George, 55, 197

Bourque, Phil, 81

Bourque, Ray, 2, 28, 55, 190

Bower, Johnny, 128, 144, 175, 207–208

Bowman, Ralph, 61

Bowman, Scotty, 46, 88, 144, 148, 218–219

Brashear, Donald, 115

Brewer, Carl, 19, 72, 78

Brimsek, Frank, 30

Broadbent, Punch, 55

Broda, Turk, 206–207

Broderick, Len and Ken, 107

Brodeur, Martin, 95–96, 103, 205–206

Brophy, Frank, 92, 108

Brophy, John, 130

Broten, Neal, 156

Brown, Andy, 29

Bruneteau, Mud, 205

Bucyk, Johnny, 87, 157

Bullard, Mike, 154

Bure, Pavel, 28, 146, 164, 202

Bure, Valeri, 62

Burke, Marty, 119

Burke, Sean, 100

Burns, Charlie, 146

Burns, Pat, 6, 148

C

Carey, Jim, 64

Carpenter, Bob, 153

Carson, Jimmy, 152–153

Cashman, Wayne, 70

Caulfield, Jay, 81

Chabot, Lorne, viii, 99, 125, 204, 205

Cheevers, Gerry, 29, 210

Chelios, Chris, 173, 190

Cherry, Don, 86, 121

Ciccarelli, Dino, 66, 113, 115, 198

Clancy, King, viii, 8, 55–56, 61

Clapper, Dit, 57–58, 70, 100

Clark, Wendel, 89

Cleghorn, Odie, 141, 142

Cleghorn, Sprague, 114

Cloutier, Real, 63

Coffey, Paul, 57, 81, 152, 155, 163, 173

Colville, Neil, 41

Conacher, Charlie, 8–9, 119, 167

Conacher, Roy, 167

Connell, Alex, 5, 61, 107

Connelly, Wayne, 204

Cote, Sylvain, 86

Cotton, Baldy, 9

Coulter, Art, 53

Cournoyer, Yvan, 189

Coutu, Billy, 114

Cowley, Bill, 164
Crozier, Roger, 102

D

Daigle, Alexandre, 15, 45
Dandurand, Leo, 214
Datsyuk, Pavel, 189
Davidson, John, 31
Day, Hap, 6
Delmore, Andy, 197
Demers, Jacques, 16, 113, 148
Denis, Marc, 97
Denneny, Corbett, 196
Denneny, Cy, 5, 55, 166, 196, 219
Desjardins, Eric, 198
Dillon, Cecil, 60
Dionne, Marcel, 20, 69, 155, 158, 162
Donnelly, Gord, 80
Dorey, Jim, 79
Douglas, Kent, 175–176
Dryden, Dave, 107
Dryden, Ken, 85, 107, 176, 210, 212
Duguay, Ron, 27
Dumart, Woody, 69
Duncan, Art, 201
Dupont, Andre, 44, 80
Durbano, Steve, 80
Durnan, Bill, 106–107, 201
Dutton, Red, 30
Dye, Babe, 201

E

Eriksson, Roland, 86
Esposito, Phil, 31, 64, 68, 70, 87,
108, 110, 125, 154, 156, 163, 166,
184, 200
Esposito, Tony, 95, 108

F

Federko, Bernie, 200
Fedorov, Sergei, 17, 21, 46, 64
Ference, Brad, 78
Ferguson, John, 135, 200
Fetisov, Slava, 46, 189
Fischer, Jiri, 193
Flett, Bill, 53
Fleury, Theo, 28, 167
Fontinato, Lou, 75, 78, 147
Forbes, Jake, 5, 19
Forsberg, Peter, 45, 165, 168,
188, 200
Forslund, Gustav, 50
Francis, Emile, 30, 85, 114
Francis, Ron, 88
Fredrickson, Frank, 214
Froese, Bob, 31
Ftorek, Robbie, 219
Fuhr, Grant, 94–95, 104, 110,
174, 207

G

Gadsby, Bill, 140, 159
Gainor, Dutch, 70
Gallinger, Don, 113
Gamble, Bruce, 144
Gardiner, Charlie, 107, 126,
208–209
Gartner, Mike, 66

Gatherum, Dave, 99

Geoffrion, Bernie, 54, 84, 125–126, 189

Gerard, Eddie, 55

Giacomin, Ed, 99,

Giguere, Jean-Sebastien, 82, 206

Gilbert, Rod, 75

Gillies, Clark, 187

Gilmour, Doug, 89, 200, 215

Glover, Fred, 140

Goldsworthy, Bill, 200

Gomez, Scott, 50, 188

Gorman, Tommy, 145, 218

Gottselig, Johnny, 51

Gradin, Thomas, 100

Gretzky, Wayne, vii, 6, 11, 55, 58, 67–68, 70, 77, 84, 87, 124–126, 152–155, 157–159, 163–167, 170–171, 172–173, 178, 180, 193, 200–202

Grier, Mike, 116

Guidolin, Bep, 53

Gunn, Roydun, 32

H

Hadfield, Vic, 29, 74

Hainsworth, George, 100, 107

Hall, Glenn, 7, 106, 210

Hall, Joe, 74, 194

Harkness, Ned, 91

Harper, Terry, 20, 135

Harris, Smokey, 9

Hart, Cecil, 170

Hartley, Bob, 217

Hartsburg, Craig, 53

Harvey, Doug, 13, 146, 173, 189

Hasek, Dominik, 94, 171, 174, 192, 195, 205, 208–209

Hatcher, Kevin, 62, 86

Heatley, Dany, 21, 177

Hedberg, Anders, 52

Hejduk, Milan, 167–168

Hewitt, Mel, 32

Hextall, Ron, 26, 102, 105, 207

Hill, Mel, 197

Hillman, Larry, 191

Hitchcock, Ken, 149

Hitchman, Lionel, 33, 114

Hlinka, Ivan, 100

Hodge, Ken, 31, 70, 153

Hoene, Phil, 61

Hoffinger, Val, 51

Hogosta, Goran, 106

Holt, Randy, 79

Homes, Harry, 4

Horner, Red, 72

Horvath, Bronco, 142

Housley, Phil, 159

Howe, Gordie, 11, 16, 21, 40, 57–58, 68–69, 71, 90–91, 124, 133, 155, 157–159, 163, 171, 191, 199–200

Howe, Mark and Marty, 58

Hrudey, Kelly, viii, 123

Huddy, Charlie, 202

Hull, Bobby, 14, 26, 43, 52, 66, 68, 87, 125, 152, 157, 164, 168
Hull, Brett, 60, 66–67, 157, 167–168, 195
Hull, Dennis, 87
Hunter, Dale, 72, 159

I

Iafrate, Al, 86
Iginla, Jarome, 161–162
Imlach, Punch, 20, 144–145, 150
Ingarfield, Earl, 62
Irvin, Dick, 218–219
Ivan, Tommy, 142

J

Jackson, Busher, 8–9, 119
Jagr, Jaromir, 17, 22, 57, 63, 87, 153, 162, 165, 171
Jensen, Steve, 86
Johnson, Brent, 205
Johnson, Tom, 189
Johnson, Virgil, 201
Johnston, Eddie, 79, 102
Joseph, Curtis, 95
Juneau, Joe, 176

K

Kallur, Anders, 192
Karakas, Mike, 6, 61
Karalahti, Jere, 111
Keane, Mike, 191

Kelly, Bob, 44, 80
Kelly, Red, 143, 172, 178, 186
Kerr, Davey, viii, 125
Kloucek, Tomas, 62
Klymkiv, Julian, 121
Konstantinov, Vladimir, 46, 182
Kovalchuk, Ilya, 21, 177
Kovalenko, Andrei, 42
Kozlov, Slava, 46, 189
Krivokrasov, Sergei, 60
Kromm, Bobby, 147
Kruse, Paul, 122
Kurri, Jari, 67, 87, 153, 156–158, 167–168, 202
Kwong, Larry, 50

L

Lach, Elmer, 70
Lafleur, Guy, 85, 163, 187, 191
LaFontaine, Pat, 163
Langdon, Darren, 122
Langkow, Daymond, 103
Langway, Rod, 33, 173
Lapointe, Guy, 85
Larionov, Igor, 46, 189
Larmer, Steve, 77
Larouche, Pierre, 66. 152–153
Leach, Reggie, 199
Leetch, Brian, 21, 24, 179
Lefebvre, Sylvain, 188
Legwand, David, 62
Lehman, Hugh, 201

Leighton, Michael, 100

Lemaire, Jacques, 44, 46, 196, 218

Lemieux, Claude, 15, 180, 191

Lemieux, Mario, vii, 24, 58, 59, 64, 67, 76, 81, 87–89, 123, 153–154, 159, 163, 170, 172, 179, 198

Leswick, Tony, 196

Leveille, Normand, 2

Lidstrom, Nicklas, 28, 178–179

Lindbergh, Pelle, 31

Lindros, Eric, 24, 45, 165

Lindsay, Ted, 19, 40, 71–73, 182

Litzenberger, Ed, 176, 192

Loob, Hakan, 153

LoPresti, Sam, 30, 94

Low, Ron, 97

Lumley, Harry, 97, 142, 207, 209

Lund, Pentti, 50

Lynn, Vic, 56

M

MacInnis, Al, 182

MacKay, Mickey, 190

MacLean, Paul, 98

MacTavish, Craig, 27, 112

Mahovlich, Frank, 2, 66

Malarchuk, Clint, 105

Malone, Joe, 38, 60–61, 64, 66, 162, 167

Maloney, Dan, 20

Maloney, Don, 110

Maniago, Cesare, 152

March, Mush, 208

Marsh, Brad, 160

Marshall, Donnie, 13

Martin, Rick, 130

Maruk, Denis, 67

Masterton, Bill, 55

Matheson, Godfrey, 143

May, Brad, 80

McAuley, Ken, 83, 98

McCool, Frank, 176, 206, 209

McKenney, Don, 49

McLean, Kirk, 6, 62, 97

McMahon, Mike, 75

McNeil, Gerry, 210

McSorley, Marty, 115

Meloche, Gilles, 97

Messier, Mark, 24, 55, 188, 192

Mikita, Stan, 2, 26, 33, 40, 51, 87, 165–166

Millen, Greg, 94, 98

Miller, Bob, 86

Miller, Kelly, 62

Mironov, Boris, 42

Mogilny, Alexander, 51, 67, 153, 156, 167

Mondou, Armand, 100

Moore, Dickie, 84

Morenz, Howie, 48, 137, 214

Morris, Bernie, 213

Morrow, Ken, 193

Mosienko, Bill, 70

Mowers, Johnny, 175

Muldoon, Pete, 40
Mullen, Joe, 65–66, 157–158
Mummery, Harold, 108, 192
Munro, Dunc, 193
Murdoch, Don, 64, 110
Murphy, Ron, 125
Murzyn, Dana, 42

N

Nabokov, Evgeni, 103
Nash, Rick, 16
Nattress, Ric, 110
Nechaev, Viktor, 51
Nedved, Petr, 24
Neilson, Roger, 140, 144, 184
Nesterenko, Eric, 87
Niedermayer, Rob and Scott, 193
Nieuwendyk, Joe, 191
Nighbor, Frank, 55, 170
Nilan, Chris, 78–79
Nilsson, Kent, 105, 156
Nilsson, Ulf, 52

O

O'Brien, Dennis, 56
O'Ree, Willie, 49
O'Reilly, Terry, 73, 75, 135
Oates, Adam, 55, 159
Odelein, Lyle, 103
Olausson, Fredrik, 208
Olcyzk, Ed, 188
Olmstead, Bert, 189

Orr, Bobby, 14, 20, 54, 58, 62–63, 68, 71, 74, 124, 147, 155, 162–163, 166, 169–171, 173, 183–184, 197
Owen, George, 27

P

Paiement, Wilf, 77
Parent, Bernie, 29, 31–33, 96, 102, 179
Paris, John Jr., 141
Park, Brad, 27
Patrick, Craig, 53
Patrick, Frank, 133, 145, 201
Patrick, Glenn, 53
Patrick, Lester, 53, 126, 133, 142, 145–146, 150, 201, 214
Patrick, Lynn, viii, 53, 144, 146
Patrick, Muzz, 53
Perreault, Gilbert, 66, 130
Persson, Stefan, 192
Petit, Michel, 57
Pettinger, Gord, 190
Picard, Robert, 14
Pilote, Pierre, 173
Pirus, Alex, 86
Pitre, Didier, 61
Plante, Jacques, 28, 30, 96, 107, 171, 174, 185, 210
Polonich, Denis, 77
Potvin, Denis, 158, 186
Potvin, Felix, 89, 94
Pratt, Babe, 113, 196

Primeau, Joe, 8, 118

Probert, Bob, 12, 110–111

Pronger, Chris, 171

Pronovost, Marcel, 7

Pudas, Albert, 50

Pulford, Bob, 135, 207–208

Q

Quackenbush, Bill, 178

Quinn, Dan, 81

Quinn, Pat, 80, 90

R

Racicot, Andre, 52

Ramage, Rob, 102

Ramsay, Craig, 56

Ratelle, Jean, 155

Ray, Rob, 73, 80

Reardon, Ken and Terry, 193

Reay, Billy, 217

Reece, Dave, 65, 93

Reese, Jeff, 104

Regan, Larry, 140

Reichel, Robert, 104

Rheaume, Manon, 50, 125

Rhodes, Damian, 103

Ricci, Mike, 62

Richard, Henri, 13, 189

Richard, Maurice, 2, 5, 7, 16, 44, 70, 71–72, 80, 84, 124, 127, 151, 153, 156, 166, 189, 197–199

Richardson, Luke, 115

Richter, Mike, 202

Riendeau, Vincent, 52

Ripley, Vic, 85

Ritchie, Dave, 60

Roach, John Ross, 19, 106

Robert, Rene, 130

Roberts, Gary, 76, 104

Roberts, Gordie, 159

Robertson, Earl, 30, 210

Robinson, Larry, 85, 190–191, 219

Rollins, Al, 172

Ross, Art, 26, 60, 141

Roy, Patrick, 94–96, 101, 157, 179, 203–205, 207–208, 216

Ruel, Claude, 91, 210

Rutherford, Jim, 64, 101

S

Sakic, Joe, 17, 91, 156, 200

Saleski, Don, 80

Salming, Borje, 48, 64, 110, 160

Sanderson, Derek, 14, 27

Saskamoose, Fred, 49

Sather, Glen, 31, 152

Savage, Reggie, 61

Savard, Denis, 77, 138, 154

Savard, Serge, 85

Sawchuk, Terry, 95–96, 99, 101, 117, 142, 144, 175, 204

Schmidt, Milt, 69, 141

Schultz, Dave, 44, 71, 73, 76–78, 80

Secord, Al, 77, 154

Selanne, Teemu, 67, 175–176

Shack, Eddie, 43, 128

Shanahan, Brendan, 76

Sharpley, Glen, 86

Sheehy, Neal, 31

Sheppard, Ray, 65

Shero, Fred, viii, 80, 96, 142–143, 147, 219

Shore, Eddie, 27, 39, 72, 100, 171

Shtalenkov, Mikhail, 42

Shutt, Steve, 85

Siebert, Babe, 104

Simmer, Charlie, 69

Simmons, Don, 108, 141

Simon, Chris, 115–116

Simpson, Craig, 152

Sinisalo, Ilkka, 61

Sittler, Darryl, 65, 93, 143

Sjoberg, Lars-Erik, 52

Skidmore, Paul, 98

Skudra, Peter, 103

Slegr, Jiri, 193

Smail, Doug, 98

Smart, Alex, 63

Smith, Billy, 75, 102, 106, 174

Smith, Clint, 70

Smith, Gary, 64, 101

Smith, Normie, 210

Stanfield, Fred, 29

Stanley, Allan, 207

Stastny, Peter, 46, 154, 156, 158, 164

Stastny, Marian, 46

Stastny, Anton, 46

Steen, Thomas, 33

Stevens, Kevin, 76, 88, 111, 154

Stevens, Scott, 20–21

Stewart, Gaye, 177

Stewart, Nels, 66, 162

Suhonen, Alpo, 146

Sullivan, Red, 7

Sundin, Mats, 91

Sutter, Brian, 145–146

Sutter, Darryl, 145–146, 149

Sutter, Dwayne, 145–146

T

Tanguay, Alex, 168

Tarasov, Anatoly, 143

Taylor, Billy, 113

Taylor, Cyclone, 126

Taylor, Dave, 69

Thomas, Steve, 64

Thompson, Paul, 30, 46, 108

Thompson, Tiny, 60, 103, 108, 141, 204, 208–209

Thornton, Joe, 21

Tibbets, Billy, 112

Tkachuk, Keith, 17, 76, 167–168

Tocchet, Rick, 88

Tootoo, Jordin, 47

Toppazzini, Jerry, 49, 108

Trottier, Bryan, 165, 186–187

Trotz, Barry, 150
Tugnutt, Ron, 94
Turnbull, Ian, 64
Tuttle, Steve, 105

U

Ubriaco, Gene, 81
Ullman, Norm, 114

V

Vadnais, Carol, 62
Vanbiesbrouck, John, 95, 153
Verbeek, Pat, 73
Vernon, Mike, 180
Vezina, Georges, 48, 98, 126, 173–174

W

Walker, Scott, 10
Watson, Bryan, 73
Weiland, Cooney, 70
Westlund, Tommy, 193
Wharram, Kenny, 87
White, Bill, 27
Whitney, Ray, 55
Wickenheiser, Doug, 138
Williams, Tiger, 72–74, 78
Winkler, Hal, 99, 205, 208–209
Worrell, Peter, 78, 116
Worsley, Gump, 97, 177, 210
Worters, Roy, 100, 107, 142

X, Y, Z

Yashin, Alexei, 19
Young, Howie, 78
Yzerman, Steve, vii, 52, 58, 157, 167, 182